W9-BUX-351

Sternwheelers & Sidewheelers

The Romance of Steamdriven Paddleboats in Canada

1333—HARBOR MONTREAL

Sternwheelers & Sidewheelers

The Romance of Steamdriven Paddleboats in Canada
by Dr. Peter Charlebois

NC PRESS LIMITED, TORONTO, 1978

Cover Design: Emma Hesse

Canadian Cataloging in Publication Data

Charlebois, Peter, 1928 —
   Sternwheelers and Sidewheelers

Bibliography: p.
Includes index.
ISBN 0-919600-73-5 bd. ISBN 0-919600-72-7 pa.

I. Paddlesteamers — History. 2. Steam Navigation — Canada — History.
I. Title.

VM311.P3C53   386'.22'40971   C77-001701-0

We would like to thank the Ontario Arts Council and the Canada Council for
their assistance in the production of this book.

New Canada Publications, a division of NC Press Limited, Box 4010, Station A,
Toronto, Ontario, M5W 1H8. (416) 368-1165.

Contents

Sam McGee, Lady Elgin, and the Road to Mandalay

Progress has swept away a romantic era in the history of Canadian transportation. Gone are the days of the mighty steamer, black smoke belching from its funnel, frothing waves at its prow, live white steam, searing, hissing and whooshing out of valves at over one hundred pounds' pressure.

No more great twenty-foot paddle wheels, thrashing against the water, responding to a surge of power from steam engines whose red-hot glowing fireboxes would burn a cord of wood in an hour, or a ton of coal, shovelled in continually by sweating firemen, in four.

In this book we will relive these vanished days. Sternwheelers have been celebrated in poetry and song.

Many people are familiar with the stern-wheeler, *Olive May*, although they may not recognize it by name. Around 1900, a Doctor Sugden was asked by the North West Mounted Policeman posted at Tagis, in the Yukon, to go to the area of Lake Labèrge to see if he could help a miner who was supposed to be sick with scurvy. After many days of travel over frozen wasteland, he arrived at the miner's shack to find him dead.

Not wishing to leave the man's body where it could be attacked by the wolves or bears, and being unable to dig a grave because of the frozen ground, Doctor Sugden loaded the miner's body onto his sleigh. On the way back, the small funeral cortege passed the *Olive May*, which was frozen in the ice near the shore of Lake Labèrge. Here was the solution. Dr. Sugden stoked up the boilers until the fire roared, and put the body in the firebox and cremated it.

A few years later he told this story to Robert W. Service, a young bank clerk, who was working in Dawson City. And around 1907, Service wrote the poem "The Cremation of Sam McGee."

Till I came to the marge of Lake Lebarge,
   and a derelict there lay;
It was jammed in the ice, but I saw in a trice
   it was called the "Alice May."
And I looked at it, and I thought a bit,
   and I looked at my frozen chum;
Then "Here," said I, with a sudden cry,
   "is my cre-ma-tor-eum."

Some planks I tore from the cabin floor,
   and I lit the boiler fire;
Some coal I found that was lying around,
   and I heaped the fuel higher;
The flames just soared, and the furnace roared —
   such a blaze you seldom see;
And I burrowed a hole in the glowing coal,
   and I stuffed in Sam McGee.

Then I made a hike,
   for I didn't like to hear him sizzle so;
And the heavens scowled, and the huskies howled,
   and the wind began to blow.
It was icy cold, but the hot sweat rolled
   down my cheeks, and I don't know why;
And the greasy smoke in an inky cloak
   went streaking down the sky.

I do not know how long in the snow
   I wrestled with grisly fear;
But the stars came out and they danced about
   ere again I ventured near;
I was sick with dread, but I bravely said:
   "I'll just take a peep inside.
I guess he's cooked, and it's time I looked";
   . . . then the door I opened wide.

And there sat Sam, looking cool and calm,
   in the heart of the furnace roar;
And he wore a smile you could see a mile,
   and he said: "Please close that door.
It's fine in here, but I greatly fear
   you'll let in the cold and storm —
Since I left Plumtree, down in Tennessee,
   it's the first time I've been warm."

Rudyard Kipling's "Mandalay" immortalizes a sidewheeler, the British warship, *Chunkin*.

By the old Moulmein Pagoda,
   lookin' eastward to the sea,
There's a Burma girl a-settin',
   an' I know she thinks o' me;
For the wind is in the palm-trees,
   an' the temple-bells they say:
"Come you back, you British soldier:
   come you back to Mandalay!"

Come you back to Mandalay,
Where the old Flotilla lay:
Can't you 'ear their PADDLES CHUNKIN'
   from
Rangoon to Mandalay?
O the road to Mandalay,
Where the flyin'-fishes play,
An' the dawn comes up like thunder outer
China 'crost the Bay!

The tragic sinking of the sidewheeler *Lady Elgin* was memorialized in a song, now forgotten, but sung at family gatherings and social occasions for many years in central Canada.

Over 100 years ago a young sailor, Alexander Farquharson, while in the middle of Lake Michigan, noticed a box floating in the water. He was able to retrieve it and bring it into his sailboat. Inside were six clocks. Later he learned that it was part of the last cargo ever carried by the *Lady Elgin*.

The *Lady Elgin* was a wooden-hulled paddlewheeler, three hundred feet long. Built in Buffalo in 1851, it was one of the most elegantly-appointed passenger boats on the lakes at that time. It had been named after the wife of Lord Elgin, Canada's Governor-General from 1847 to 1854.

Early in September, 1860, the *Lady Elgin* was chartered by an Irish group from Milwaukee for a trip to Chicago to hear a political speech by Stephen A. Douglas, Abraham Lincoln's opponent in the 1860 presidential campaign. The three hundred men and women spent the day of September 7 listening to political speeches and in the evening they reboarded the ship and were entertained by a German brass band. The ship had not been out on the lake very long before it encountered a thunderstorm and a north-east gale.

About 2:30 a.m., as they were steaming north off Waukegan, the ship was struck on the port side just after the paddle box. Captain Wilson ran on deck to see a lumber-laden schooner, the *Augusta*, along side. It had rammed the *Lady Elgin*. Rough waters soon separated the two vessels forever.

Captain Wilson, believing any damage to his ship would be slight, had a boat lowered to put a canvas patch over the hole. But the boat soon fell far behind the steamer. It was then discovered that the hole in the hull extended well below the water line and that it would need more than canvas to stop the water rushing in. To lighten his ship, the Captain ordered two hundred cattle aboard jettisoned and directed his course towards shore, ten miles to the west. In the engine room, the pumps worked frantically, but the rising water soon extinguished the boiler fires and the ship lost way.

Captain Wilson ordered the life boats launched but succeeded in lowering only two into the water. The life preservers were two-inch hardwood planks, five feet long and eighteen inches wide. Apparently, none of them were ever used. One of the surviving officers told of seeing women passengers huddled together in the ballroom, absolutely mute.

As the water rose within her hull, the *Lady Elgin* listed more and more until the engines broke loose and tore through the hull. In less than half an hour after the collision, the beautiful *Lady Elgin* slid towards the bottom of Lake Michigan. As it sank, the hurricane deck broke loose and many of the almost four hundred people aboard clung to it until it broke up. Wilson encouraged his passengers and crew to fight for their lives as they clung to bits of wreckage in the darkness. The drummer of the German band, Charles Beverung, used his large base drum as a life preserver and so saved himself. Nearly all the members of the band reached an island near the scene of the sinking.

When daylight came, those who survived were within a hundred feet of the steep banks along Winnetka, now a residential suburb of Chicago. Although the land was so near, salvation was not. The north-west wind rode great breakers onto the shore and only thirty of the shipwrecked passengers made it through the great undertow alive.

Of the four hundred persons on the ship at least three hundred and two were lost. Up to this time, this was the worst disaster on the Great Lakes.

The *Augusta* reached Chicago with difficulty, but safely. Its captain, Captain Malott, was arrested, but absolved of blame after an investigation, as were the crew and owners of the *Lady Elgin*. The judgement was based on a law that not only gave sail the right of way over steam, but did not require sailing vessels to carry running lights. Apparently the *Augusta* had sighted the passenger steamer twenty minutes before the collision but in the rain had misjudged the distance between them.

Four years after the disaster, in 1864, a new ruling was made requiring sailing vessels to carry running lights. Since there were still nearly 1,900 ships under sail by 1870 the regulations were long overdue.

Lost on the Lady Elgin

Up from the poor man's cottage,
* Forth from the mansion door,*
Sweeping across the water,
* And echoing along the shore,*
Borne on the morning breezes,
* Swept by the evening gale,*
Cometh a voice of mourning,
* A sad and solemn wail.*

*   * * ***

CHORUS:

Lost on the Lady Elgin,
* Sleeping to wake no more,*
Numbered with those three hundred
* Who failed to reach the shore.*

*   * * ***

The Lady Elgin *in the Port of Chicago just before its last voyage. K. E. Thro Collection.*

The Early Development of Paddlewheel Steamboats

Long before time was measured, man was devising means to speed his passage over the water's surface. First a log, then a raft, then canoes and paddles, and finally sails. Until the eighteenth century, all marine construction was only a variation of the principles discovered and used thousands of years before.

Seagoing sailboats plied the eastern Mediterranean as early as 5,000 B.C., and by 2,000 B.C. the basic problems of ship building had been solved. By Roman times galleys over one hundred feet long were routinely constructed, and, as the ships grew larger, more decks were fitted into the hulls. In 264 B.C., Appius Claudius transported his army across the Straits of Messina in boats powered by paddlewheels turned by capstans. A painting by Raphael in 1514 entitled "Galatea" shows a sea nymph in a boat being towed by a dolphin: the side of the boat clearly has auxiliary paddlewheels.

The last years of the seventeenth century saw the development of a rudimentary steam engine and the next century its application to marine engineering. The first successful side paddle steamboat was the *Pyroscaphe,* built in France in 1783, and used on the Saone River near Lyon. The first commercially successful steamboat, to our knowledge, was the *Charlotte Dundas* built in 1801 at Grangemouth, Scotland, as a tug to haul barges on the Forth and Clyde Canal and the Clyde River. It was fifty-six feet long and eight feet deep, with an eighteen foot beam, and was driven by a stern paddle ten feet in diameter. It was powered by a Watt engine of about ten horsepower.

Staunch was the noble steamer,
  Precious the freight she bore,
Gayly she loosed her cable
  A few short hours before.
Grandly she swept the harbor,
  Joyful she rang her bell,
Little thought we ere morning
  To toll so sad a knell.

* * *

All o'er the land is mourning,
  Weeping for parents gone;
Children who slept at evening
  Woke orphans at the dawn.
Sisters for brothers calling;
  Husbands for missing wives;
Such were the ties that were severed
  By those three hundred lives.

The next commercially successful steamboat was the *Clermont,* built by Robert Fulton in 1807 and operated on the Hudson River in New York State. That same year, the first seagoing steamship, the *Phoenix,* was built.

Robert Fulton, because he persisted in building them, is called the father of steamboats. He was born on a farm in Lancaster County, Pennsylvania, in 1765. At the age of eight he was apprenticed to a jeweller. In his early teens he went to art school in London, England. It was there that he first became acquainted with steam engines. Fulton soon produced inventions pertaining to canal locks, submarines, and steamboats. His first steam engine, built in 1803, was so heavy that it broke through the bottom of the boat.

By August, 1807, the *Clermont* was ready for trial. It had a single cylinder, condensing steam engine with a piston diameter of twenty-four inches and a four-foot stroke which drove two fifteen-foot side paddle wheels. It made the one hundred and fifty mile run from New York to Albany in thirty-two hours, averaging four miles per hour.

In 1812, the *Comet* was launched on the Clyde River in Scotland. It was the first commercially successful merchant steamboat in Europe and attained a speed of 6.7 knots while operating between Glasgow and Greenock.

Terminology

As boat and engine-building technology developed, new words were introduced into the language and use was made of terms which were formerly applied to sailing ships. The front of the boat was the "bow": the back the "stern." A boat powered by a rotating paddle at its back was known as a "sternwheeler"; one with rotating paddles on its side, a "sidewheeler." A boat powered by a propeller was termed a "screw ship" because of the rotating action of the propeller blades. The boat's length was still referred to as "length" but the boat's width was measured at its widest and was termed the "beam."

The weight of boats is expressed either in "gross tons" or "tons displacement." One gross ton is 2,240 pounds. Gross tons refers to the total weight of the hull, engines and superstructure. "Tons displacement" refers to the weight of water the hull of a vessel displaces when it floats in the water.

The various platforms placed within the hull were termed "decks," with the main deck being that one which was level with the upper edge of the hull of the boat. If the back of the boat was rounded, this area of the main deck was known as the "fan tail" as it resembled a fan and was at the end or tail of the boat. It was always a favourite lounging area for passengers. As the decks rose above the main deck, they were numbered either with numerals or letters. The last or topmost deck was referred to as the "upper deck" and at its forward or bow end stood the "pilot" or wheelhouse, a small glassed-in cabin from which the captain and the helmsman guided the ship.

The wheelhouse was built at the front of the topmost deck, usually the third level, near the smokestacks. These were always tall, protruding well above the boat, so the hot ashes, cinders and other burning lumps of fuel would not fall back upon the vessel as happened to the disabled *Northcote* at Batoche in 1885.

In the early steamboats the passenger cabins were quite small and grouped in the same area of the deck. Usually they had one small vertical window for ventilation and light. The cargo or baggage area was on a lower deck with large access doors for easy loading from the docks. If you look at a photograph of a steamboat, you can easily determine whether it was a freighter or a passenger boat, or both, by counting the cabin windows and the cargo doors.

Above the main deck was often a "saloon" deck, having a few staterooms and a dining room; these were fitted up for the better-paying passengers. On the saloon deck, also, there would be a separate bathroom for the men, and for the women. In the very early steamboats there might be a large bunkhouse-type room on one end of the boat for men, and a smaller on the other end, for the women.

To make more money, the ship owners very often would sell a bar concession. Some of these trips must have been quite an event. Rough-and-ready miners, travelling along a humid river on a hot day, in a crowded, boring, confined, oppressively hot boat would have been eager customers.

The Development of Steam Engines

For thousands of years until 1800, boats were propelled by sails and hand-driven oars. In the relatively short period of one hundred years after James Watt improved the steam engine, sails became obsolete.

In 1690, Denis Papin built, in France, a model of a practical steam engine. Commercial versions were built in England by Thomas Savery in 1698 and by Thomas Newcomen in 1715 to pump water from deep mine shafts.

This is a sketch of Papin's model:

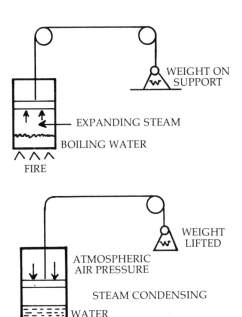

A small quantity of water was poured into a 2½ inch diameter cylinder. A sliding piston was placed in the top of the cylinder and the water was heated to boiling. Steam pressure raised the piston to the top of the cylinder. The flame was removed and as the steam condensed, a partial vacuum was created, causing the piston to fall and the weight to be raised.

Savery used a separate "boiler" to raise the steam pressure and devised a valve system to admit it into the cylinder. The condensation of steam in the cylinder was speeded up by spraying the cylinder with cold water.

Newcomen further speeded up the condensation by injecting a cold water spray directly into the cylinder.

James Watt, perhaps the greatest name in steam engine development, made many other design improvements. He realized that a great deal of heat was being lost in heating the cylinder in order to fill it with steam and then in cooling it for condensation. He solved the problem by connecting to the cylinder a separate vessel, a "condenser" to condense the steam. In addition, an air pump was connected to the condenser to suck air out of it and improve the vacuum. The condenser was kept cool with water and the cylinder hot with steam jacketing and insulation. When the valve was opened between the cylinder and the condenser, the steam rushed into the latter and was condensed. The result was a great saving in steam consumption.

In 1782, Watt patented the "Double Action Engine." Until then, the piston performed work only on the one stroke as it was pushed outwards from the cylinder. In the double action engine, work is accomplished on the return stroke by admitting steam on the other side of the piston.

SINGLE ACTION ENGINE

DOUBLE ACTION ENGINE

In 1788, Watt designed the "centrifugal governor," which allowed the speed of rotation of a steam engine to be easily controlled. He arranged a set of weights, usually three, which rotated around a central axis attached to the flywheel of the engine. The faster the flywheel rotated, the farther away from the central axis the weights would move. Their movement then controlled a valve which governed the amount of steam entering the cylinder. The operator could control the excursion of the weights and therefore the speed of the engine.

As early as 1725 the atmospheric type steam engine had been well established. Watt's engine, fifty years later, operated at only about two pounds steam pressure. As the steam pressure was raised, the inadequate boiler systems would explode. The original boilers were metal containers, either square or kettle-shaped, initially made of copper and brass, later of iron. Gradually the boilers were improved, and by 1811 high pressure "expansive" type engines were being built to use the higher pressure steam. "Compound" engines used about half the steam required by a Watt atmospheric engine.

High pressure steam is passed into a high pressure cylinder where it acts on the piston causing low pressure steam "S" from the previous working stroke to be transferred to the low pressure cylinder for a second working stroke. The movement of the steam is controlled by valves which are not shown in the diagram.

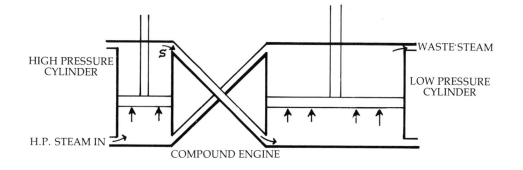

HIGH PRESSURE CYLINDER

LOW PRESSURE CYLINDER

WASTE-STEAM

H.P. STEAM IN

COMPOUND ENGINE

When using high pressure steam in an "expansive" engine maximum power is obtained by allowing steam to enter during the whole time the piston takes to move from one end to the other; however, maximum efficiency is achieved by admitting the steam for only a fraction of the stroke. When the steam inlet valve is closed the trapped steam continues to exert pressure on the piston which continues to move. With the movement of the piston the pressure drops because the steam is

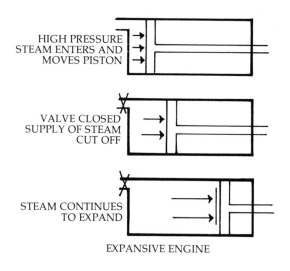

HIGH PRESSURE STEAM ENTERS AND MOVES PISTON

VALVE CLOSED SUPPLY OF STEAM CUT OFF

STEAM CONTINUES TO EXPAND

EXPANSIVE ENGINE

expanding to fill a larger space. The engine designer must achieve a balance between high power with low efficiency and low power with high efficiency.

All steam engines are basically of the same design. A fire in a firebox heats water to steam in pipes surrounded by a steel cover, known as a "boiler." The steam from the boiler is stored under pressure in a container, the "steam chest." From the steam chest, by way of a valve system, the steam is allowed as needed to enter the cylinder where it pushes against the piston. The piston, which is actually one wall of the cylinder, moves outward, doing work, with a backward and forward or "to and fro" motion.

The problem is to convert a to-and-fro motion to a rotary motion. It is simple to use rotary motion either to turn paddle wheels or a propeller.

The conversion of to-and-fro motion to rotary motion was made possible by the development of a crank mechanism and a flexible joint. The first practical engines used a beam. In "vertical beam engines," the to-and-fro motion is exerted on one end of a beam which partially rotates around a central axis. The beam moves up and down. Its opposite end is connected to a rod which projects at an

angle. The rod is attached to the circumference of a wheel in such a way that the wheel is forced to rotate as the rod moves up and down. This attachment of the rod to the wheel circumference is a "crank mechanism." The rotating wheel is in turn attached to paddle wheels or a propeller.

The crank mechanism also works other devices which open and close valves at the required time. When the piston reaches the top of the cylinder, a valve must close to stop the input of steam into the cylinder, and another valve must open to exhaust the expanded lower pressure steam.

The crank mechanism of the vertical beam engine of the Ticonderoga *at Burlington, Vermont. The up and down force in the vertical piston rod (upper right) is transferred to a rotating force by means of the horizontal arms of the crank mechanism.*

The Development of the Steamship Engine

In the early years of steam engine development, American builders favoured the vertical beam engine. The disadvantage of this model was that its use of a large heavy beam above the top deck (i.e. above the boat's centre of gravity) made the boat rather unstable. For this reason, British engineers preferred the side lever engine, in which the beam mechanism was placed within the hull, *below* the vessel's centre of gravity.

Both of these designs were gradually replaced by the inclined acting engine. This model eliminated the heavy beam and allowed for the introduction of multiple power cylinders within the hull. It was both more stable and more powerful than its forerunners.

Steam engines reached their peak of development around 1900. At that time they were able to produce over 20,000 horsepower from 200 pounds of steam. Over the years, the amount of coal required to produce 50 horsepower per hour decreased from 1,600 pounds to 75 pounds. But even the latter low consumption represents a thermal efficiency of only 20 % as compared with 25 % efficiency for a gas engine or 32 % for a diesel. For this reason, no steam engines are being built today.

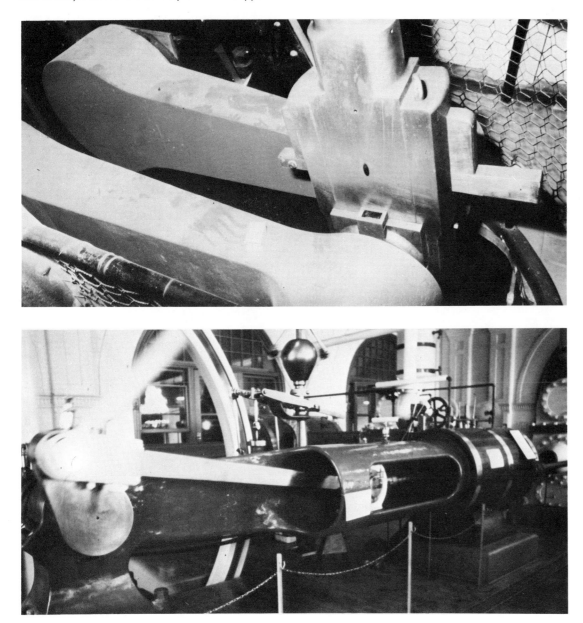

Single cylinder steam engine in the Steam Museum at Kingston, Ontario. The horizontal cylinder and piston (right) impart a to and fro motion to the piston rod (centre) which is, in turn, connected to a crank mechanism (extreme left). The to and fro motion is there converted to rotary motion, causing the flywheel in the background to turn.

The Vertical Beam Engine

This is an engineer's drawing of the vertical beam engine of a large boat. It extends from the bottom of the hull to above the top deck. The highest part, the "walking" beam, is enclosed in a cabin to protect it from the elements.

High pressure steam from the boilers is stored in a steam chest, the small vertical upright cylinder on the extreme left side of our picture, where the engineer is working the valves to let steam into the cylinder (next to it on the right). This cylinder has a diameter of up to five feet.

The top end of the cylinder is formed by the piston, not shown here because it is inside the cylinder when the beam is in this position. The piston moves up and down in the cylinder. When the piston is down, the inside volume of the cylinder is quite small. At this position the engineer must inject high pressure steam from the steam chest to get the engine started. Thereafter the valves will open and close by themselves.

The pressure now causes the piston and the rod attached to it to move upwards. When the piston reaches its maximum extension, a valve system is activated so that the steam in the cylinder is exhausted. The piston moves back down towards the bottom of the cylinder. The vertical up-and-down motion of the piston rod is transmitted to the left end of the rotating beam, which is horizontal in our picture, causing the left end of the beam to move upwards, partially rotating around its central axis.

When the left end of the beam goes up, the right end goes down. The motion of the beam is like a child's teeter-totter and to the observer, the beam appears to be "walking."

Engineer's drawing of the vertical beam engine from the steamer Puritan, *1889. Courtesy Steamship Historical Society, University of Baltimore, U.S.A.*

Vertical beam engine assembled in a shipyard prior to installation. Note method of attaching axle and paddle wheels. Courtesy Steamship Historical Society, University of Baltimore, U.S.A.

These engines are frequently called "walking beam engines" but their more technical name is "vertical beam engines" because they are vertically placed within the ship's hull.

Attached to the right end of the beam is a connecting rod which follows the up-and-down motion and is connected below by means of a crank to the axle or driveshaft (bottom right). This crank mechanism converts the to-and-fro motion of the piston to a rotary motion which causes the paddle wheel to turn.

A vertical beam engine can be seen in the *Ticonderoga* on display in Burlington, Vermont, U.S.A.

The Side Lever Engine

The side lever steam engine was designed for maximum stability. The weight of its heavy beam was carried in the hull of the ship, below the centre of gravity. The structure of the engine can be clearly seen in the illustration. When steam was injected into the large cylinder on the left, the piston was pushed up. (This piston is not visible as it is behind the rod attached to the beam.) The rod then pulled the beam up, causing it to rotate partially on its axis. The right end of the beam swung down in consequence. It in turn was attached by a crank mechanism (upper right) to an axle (to the left of the crank) which rotated the paddle wheels.

This is a sketch of the side lever engine commonly installed in British boats. Author's Private Collection.

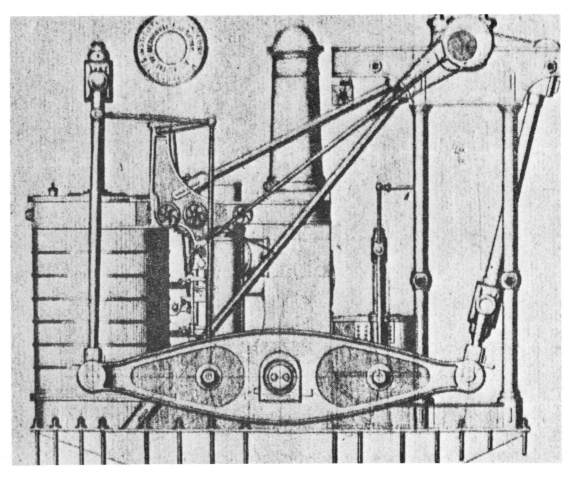

The Inclined Acting Engine

As its name suggests, this engine was built with its cylinders and piston rods acting at an inclined angle to the hull of the boat. Inclined acting engines retained basic steam engine principles. Steam was generated in boilers, then stored under high pressure in a storage space or "steam chest". From the steam chest, by means of a valve system, the steam was conducted into a power cylinder. Multiple cylinders were lined up perpendicular to the side of the ship (as shown on the left of the sketch below). The pistons were positioned within guides and supports at an angle to the ship's bottom. A crank mechanism attached these pistons to the axle (to the right of the diagram) which in turn drove the paddle wheel.

The inclined acting engine was a relatively modern invention, perfected about 1910, when it might have had as many as three power cylinders. The first or "high pressure" cylinder received steam from the steam chest at close to 100 pounds pressure, and exhausted it at approximately 60 pounds pressure into a larger cylinder/piston combination. This second cylinder exhausted the steam at 25 pounds pressure into the third, and largest, cylinder.

Engines having two power cylinders were termed "double expansion engines." Those with three were called "triple expansion."

The inclined acting engine was low and wide and could be contained within the hull of the boat. This concentration of weight below gave the boat greater stability than could the old vertical beam engines.

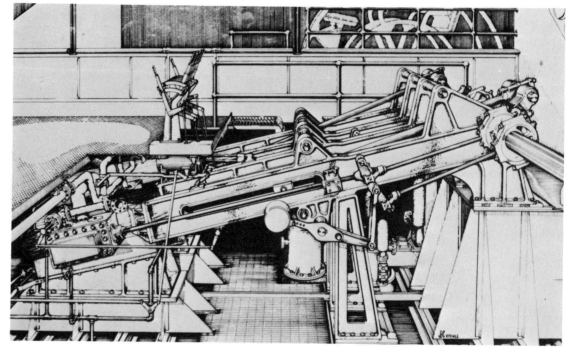

The steam storage chest of an inclined acting engine as found in the ferry Trillium *based in Toronto harbour.*

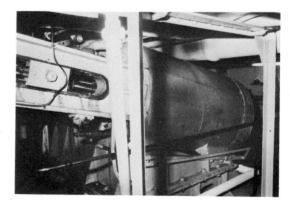

The large low pressure cylinder of the ferry Trillium *in Toronto Harbour, showing the upward inclination of the cylinder and its piston rod.*

The inclined acting engine of the ferry Trillium, showing the small high pressure cylinder and the larger low pressure cylinder. This is a double expansion engine.

Engine control room of the Trillium. The handles in the centre control valves which direct the steam to various parts of the engine.

Steam Engine Improvements

Steam engines reached their peak of development around 1900. These engines were able to produce more than twenty thousand horsepower from an initial two hundreds pounds steam pressure.

To increase the power of the engines, three routes are available and all have been used. The size of the cylinders can be kept fairly small but they may be increased in number, as in present-day automobile engines. The builders can also make an engine with only one cylinder but increase its size, as they did with the "walking beam engines" that powered steamboats in the era 1830 to 1910. The single cylinder grew to about fifty inches in diameter and the piston, when it was pushed by the expanding gas, would travel or have a "stroke" of five feet.

Power could also be increased by introducing more powerful expanding gases into the cylinder. From the original hot air, they turned to various forms of steam, under a few pounds pressure, and then to super-heated steam, under the many hundreds of pounds of pressure now used in steam turbines.

As steam engines were made more powerful, they became larger and heavier. This eventually led to the more compact diesel or gas engine. Watt's initial engine ran at two pounds steam pressure.

In 1877, the British warship *H.M.S. Iris* was given a boiler in the form of a cylinder. Cylindrical boilers produced higher steam pressure without structural failure and soon pressures of one hundred pounds were common.

One of the prices paid for jamming the safety valves of the boilers was that the boiler would eventually develop a pressure beyond its capacity and explode. When the boiler exploded, it usually killed several people and it always wrecked the boat.

On April 14th, 1861, the sternwheeler *Fort Yale* pulled out of Fort Hope B.C., to go the last fifteen miles of its regular run between New Westminster and Fort Yale. It was fully loaded with freight and passengers and was behind schedule. In this particular area, the water was very fast and there were many rapids. The steamer, not only trying to make up time, but also fighting the swift water, was actually losing ground. The Captain had ordered much more steam pressure than usual to give his engine more power.

A reporter, H. Lee Alley of the Ballouis *Express,* left a description of what happened that fateful day. He wrote: "We had been seated but a few moments when, with a great roar, the boiler blew up, scattering men and fragments of the pilot house and upper structure all over Christendom. Over eight persons were killed in this appalling disaster. A bystander claimed to have seen Captain Jamieson blown into the air, but his body was never recovered. Captain Irving, unhurt, endeavoured to beach the wreck but the steering hawser he used snapped like so much twine

This typical boiler, used to generate steam for a large steam engine, can be seen in the basement of the Steam Museum, Kingston, Ontario. The front face of the boiler has been removed showing the pipes in which the water is converted to steam.

and the partially-submerged craft was swirled down the rushing waters to a resting place on the first sand bar below Hope."

On August 14th, 1893, the boiler of the steamship *Annie Faxton* exploded. It was on its regular trip down river from Lewiston, B.C., with the bow heading upstream into the current. Captain Boughman gave the signal for full steam ahead and instantly there was a tremendous explosion.

A young man standing on the bank, waiting for the steamer, saw the explosion and is the only reliable witness. All others were either dead, in shock or unconscious. To him, the explosion was so muffled that the boat had the appearance of falling to pieces, like a cardhouse.

The purser, Mr. Tappan, a moment before, had left his new bride of two weeks seated in his office on the upper deck, and had come down with his freight book preparing to go ashore. While standing by the gangplank,

within a few feet of the boiler, he felt the shock and saw deckhands standing by his side fall dead with blood gushing from their wounds. His first thoughts were of his new wife and he turned to go to her, but on looking round, saw that the house and cabin had been blown completely out of existence and there was no longer anything there.

The Captain felt the first effects of the shock and saw, beside him, his mate, Thomas MacIntosh, who was also in the pilot house, instantly beheaded. The Captain became unconscious and recovered two hours later to find that he had been thrown onto the river bank.

Most of the bodies were terribly mutilated, but that of Mrs. Tappan, the new bride, was found without a scar, indicating that she had been stunned by the explosion, thrown into the river, and drowned.

The boiler, when last inspected, was apparently in good condition, and the Captain stated that they were carrying no more than the usual amount of steam. The fusible plug which was in the boiler, and which was subsequently found, failed to show any mark of excessive heat as it would have, had there been no water in the boiler.

When the new Dominion of Canada Steamboat Laws became effective in 1873, they required steamboats to maintain a maximum of no more than one hundred pounds steam pressure. The new laws also required the boilers to be tested every year at a pressure double their operating pressure. This was a hard law to enforce and many of the paddle wheel captains thought nothing of screwing down the safety valve and running their engines at one hundred and forty pounds pressure.

Two other limiting factors in the development of powerful steam engines were the strength of iron used in the engine castings and the strength of the hull. The maximum safe length for wooden ships was about three hundred feet. From 1850 until 1880, iron was the principal material used to strengthen hulls and later it was to fabricate completely the larger hulls. By 1885, iron, and some steel, largely replaced wood in hull construction, except for the Prairies and the north.

Stronger steels were not developed until about 1885, and nickel steel, the strongest of all, was not developed until the 1900s. Steel offered superior strength and produced a lighter, stronger hull with riveted parts. It was not until World War II that steel hulls could be completely welded without rivets.

Vertical beam engines were large, and usually had only one cylinder, which could be from two to three feet in diameter. Although the engine mechanism was relatively slow-moving, it was subjected to great strain. The parts of the early steamboat engines were made of cast iron.

The art of metallurgy was still in its infancy; the companies which cast the engine parts had no means of telling whether the interiors of their castings were defective, as they can only be examined by means of powerful x-ray machines.

Thus, one of the most frequent problems, despite all the care that was taken, was the fracture of some of the heavy iron castings which formed the engine parts. The most common components to break were the rods connecting the cylinder to the beam, and the crank attachment to the axle of the paddle wheel. There was no welding during this era and once a heavy iron casting broke, it could not be repaired. A new one had to be cast.

Sternwheelers and Sidewheelers

The development and demise of paddle-wheelers has followed the development of Canadian roads and railroads.

Sternwheelers are designed to travel in shallow, narrow rivers; therefore, whenever there was a combination of a shallow, narrow river and an insufficient road or railway system, sternwheelers were used. When roads or railways were built, the paddlewheelers could not compete economically and eventually disappeared.

Sternwheelers were constructed following the pattern of the Mississippi river boats. The hull was built like a simple rowboat, but on a larger scale. It was from three to eight feet deep, with a sharp prow and square stern, and was strengthened by many U-shaped wooden ribs to which the hull planking was attached. There were very few metal-hulled stern-wheelers, and they did not appear until the 1880s.

A majority of the hulls were between four and five feet deep and did not contain watertight bulkheads. If the hull was damaged, water would leak into the whole length of the ship. Depending on the size of the hole, the boat could very quickly sink. In later years some of the hulls of the British Columbia sternwheelers, such as the *B.X.*, were built with watertight compartments.

To keep the ship as narrow as possible, its propelling mechanism was installed at the back or stern — a paddle wheel which extended the whole width of the boat.

The engines of sidewheelers were placed in the centre of the boat. But the engines of sternwheelers were placed at either end of the main deck. In order to keep the boat well-balanced, the boilers and furnaces were for-

ward, level with the main deck. This has two advantages: the furnaces were open to the air, securing all the draught possible; and the fuel was ready at hand, piled on the front deck. When the boat stopped to take on wood, it would run its nose onto the river bank, put some planks down as a gangway, and the crew would carry wood onto the deck.

The steam was conducted, by pipes, back to the engines. What with hot furnaces and boilers in the front, the long steam pipes along the sides, and the steam being exhausted by the engine at the back, the main deck was a very hot, uncomfortable place to spend your trip. Nevertheless, if you could not pay full fare, that was where you travelled.

Sidewheel steamboats were designed much like our present-day vessels. They were deep enough for two or three deck levels and could carry hundreds of passengers and tons of freight.

Sidewheelers worked best on waters not subject to bad storms and high waves. A sidewheeler in deep waves often partially lost control as the side paddles rolled in and out of the water. However, the sidewheelers were very manoeuvrable in calm water, starting and stopping quickly. These features are needed in crowded harbours, lakes or rivers, where agility and speed are required.

Paddle Wheels

The first paddle wheels in all sidewheelers, as well as all sternwheelers, were built with the paddles bolted to the spokes of the wheel. The paddle entered and left the water at the same angle as the spoke to which it was attached. Because the paddle does not enter the water vertically, it exerts pressure onto the water in two directions, downward and backwards. Only the backward motion is useful in propelling the boat forward.

After 1885, "feathering" paddle wheels were installed in sidewheelers. They are designed so that the paddles, instead of being fixed to the arms of the wheel, move in such a way that they are always perpendicular, whether they are entering or leaving the water. All the thrust is to the stern and the efficiency of the paddle wheels is increased.

On sidewheelers, both paddle wheels usually turn in the same direction. If the boat had to have quick turning ability, it could be built with one engine governing each wheel or with a disconnect arrangement in the axle system so one paddle wheel could go ahead while the other was stopped.

The paddles, or floats, of sternwheelers are fixed to the circumference of the paddle wheel at the back of the boat. In action, they dip approximately eighteen inches into the water.

Scows

Scows were an integral part of the stern-wheeler transportation system. Sternwheelers usually pushed one or more loaded scows in front of them, doubling or even tripling their payload. Scows preceded sternwheelers, supplemented their transporting capacities, and then outlived them.

Scows were expendable, roughly built, usually only to make the trip one way. In the early days, scows were made of hand-sawn or whip-sawn lumber from timber cut on the riverbanks. But eventually, the number of scows needed was so great that power-driven sawmills were set up to turn out the necessary planks.

Scows were flexible, flat-bottomed, about fifty feet long, perhaps eight feet wide, capable of carrying up to twenty-five tons. The bow and stern were square. Planking was caulked and tarred, enough to make them relatively water-proof for at least one trip. The top would overhang the bottom for loading.

Occasionally, scows were provided with a "sweep" or steering oar, but more often they followed the current downstream. Men with poles would push them off, back into the current, should they drift into shallow water.

At mealtime, the scow would be steered to the river bank, the cook-fire set up. Originally each riverman would make his own lunch. However, in later years, when river traffic increased, a cook and a dormitory scow were provided.

The flotilla then never really stopped. The scows would be lashed together and the men

Sternwheeler, showing the paddles attached directly to the spokes of the wheel. Author's Private Collection.

sailing them would walk over to the cook and dormitory scow for their meals and rest. On clear nights, on smooth stretches of river, the flotilla would quietly drift downstream all night, the men sleeping among the boxes and bales.

At the journey's end, the scows would be sold for $10–15 or broken up for their lumber. Sometimes scows were built for more permanent use, braced with iron, and covered with iron sheeting on the bottoms. Many a paddle-wheeler, stripped of its machinery, worked out its last days converted to a scow or a barge.

Today

With the advances in diving technology present day skin divers are able to visit many of the sunken paddlewheel steamboats of long ago. They are still there and still relatively intact. Last year Dr. D. Stewart and other skin divers from Kingston visited and walked upon the decks of the old sidewheeler *Comet*. The hull, paddlewheels, engine decks and super-structure are still intact. It is resting upright on the muddy bottom of the lake halfway between Wolfe Island and Amherst Island in 85 feet of water. Because of the muddy bottom visibility is only ten feet but this and other wrecks are readily explored by local scuba diving clubs.

Shipbuilding has traditionally been an important industry in the Atlantic provinces. The reputation of the area in the nineteenth century derived from its superior construction of merchant sailing vessels, most of which were exported to Great Britain. However, from the 1830's on, a certain number of steamboats were built, and steam navigation became increasingly important until the arrival of the railroads. The first locomotive in New Brunswick arrived aboard a steamboat in 1869, heralding the beginning of the end for paddlewheelers there, as all over Canada.

The establishment of the shipbuilding trade was a direct result of the abundance of Canadian timber, and its accessibility to the coast. Supplying wood to stoke the steamboats became a lucrative sideline for farmers. But the major factor contributing to the pre-eminence of ships in the Atlantic provinces was that the waterways were often the only routes into their interiors. Many areas of Newfoundland, Nova Scotia, Prince Edward Island and New Brunswick were not serviced by road or railway. However these provinces have many rivers and large bays which are sheltered from ocean storms, and are navigable for much of the year. These quiet waters became the domain of the paddlewheelers.

It was on the Saint John River that the paddlewheelers were dominant. This river was the chief commercial transportation artery into New Brunswick. Through various tributaries and lakes, it connects every county except Gloucester. Its waters were once navigable as far as Florenceville. The famous reversing falls, though treacherous at low tide, can be safely crossed at high tide when the harbour level equals that of the river mouth. Below Fredericton, the river forms a broad estuary to meet the sea.

Steamboats first appeared on the Saint John River with the *General Stacey Smyth* in 1816. By 1900 over 65 steamers had travelled along its length; among them the *Victoria*, the *David*

A copy of a plaque commissioned by the Canadian Government, now lost. Author's Private Collection.

Weston, the *Hampton* and the *Aberdeen*. Many of the boats were sternwheelers, which were well adapted to unsophisticated facilities. Where there were no docks but the river was shallow enough, the nose of these boats could be run right onto the shore, allowing the passengers to disembark gracefully — and dryly.

Steamboats were not confined to inland waters. In the 1830's the *Royal William* sailed between the river ports and the major centres of eastern Canada and the United States. Designed to travel between Québec and Halifax, it became the first "British" steamboat to dock at Boston, Massachusetts, and later the first boat to cross the Atlantic under its own steam. The *Heather Belle* hugged the coast of Prince Edward Island, and the *Fawn* ferried passengers between St. John and Fredericton.

Although the early steamboats were efficient they were not always safe, and the Atlantic provinces have their share of tragic stories. The most notorious misadventure involving a steamboat was not due to poor technology but human malice. One weekend, the Captain of the *Ben Bevridge* threw his drunken engineer into jail to sober him up. The following Monday morning the police delivered the engineer, furious and hungover, to his ship. He proceeded to sabotage the engine by readjusting the weight on the safety valve and stoking up the furnaces. Pressure increased in the boilers and they blew up. Another ship, the *James D. Pierce*, picked up the survivors of the blast. Among them was the engineer. He hid until they reached Woodstock, where he made good his escape into Maine.

The *Royal William* was built for the Québec and Halifax Steam Navigation Company by the Black and Campbell Company of Québec City. The machinery was built in Scotland and was finished and installed by the Bennett Henderson Company of Montréal. The wooden hull was 160 feet long, 28 feet wide and 18 feet deep. Construction was begun in September, 1830, and the *Royal William* was launched on April 27, 1831.

The two side lever engines had cylinders 51 inches in diameter with a five-foot stroke and operated under a steam pressure of four to five pounds. The paddle wheels were 19 feet in diameter. The *Royal William*, as with other steamships of this era, was basically a sailing vessel with an auxiliary steam engine. By 1850, the new vessels being built were steamboats with auxiliary sails.

The *Royal William*, which was named after William IV of Great Britain, provided 50 berths in the lower deck and accommodation for 80 passengers in steerage. The dining room was located in the roundhouse on the upper deck.

The *Royal William* made three round trips in 1831 between Québec, St. Lawrence River ports, New Brunswick, and Nova Scotia.

On June 17, 1833, the *Royal William* was the first British steamer to enter the port of Boston, Massachusetts. There, it was inspected by U.S. President Andrew Jackson. The newspapers commented on the dismal black paint of the ship's exterior! It left on June 23, 1833, for the return trip to Halifax and Québec City.

Because many of the sea ports were closed during the cholera epidemic of 1832, the owners of the *Royal William* had sustained very severe financial losses. They decided that they would have to offer the ship for sale in London, England. It left Pictou, Nova Scotia, on August 18, 1833, loaded with 324 tons of coal, bound for London. However, very early

in the trip, the starboard engine became disabled and the steamer had to struggle along on its port engine, assisted by sails. As with many early boats, the *Royal William* burned so much fuel that on a long trip it required an accompanying auxiliary vessel to carry extra fuel.

A common problem at this time was the encrustation of salt from sea water in the boilers. This encrustation became so thick that it was necessary to stop the engines every four days and clean the boilers. Later, this problem was solved by distilling the salt out of the sea water before using it in the boiler.

On September 6, 1833, the *Royal William* steamed into the Isle of Wight, the first Canadian steamship to cross the Atlantic. It was purchased by the Spanish Government in

The Royal William *was equipped with both sails and paddle wheels. Archives Nationales du Québec.*

September, 1834, renamed the *Isabella Segunda*, given a battery of guns and equipped as a corvette. It was the first steamer of the Spanish Navy in active war service.

In 1840, the ship was sent to Bordeaux, France, for overhauling and refitting. However, the timbers were so badly rotted that the vessel was useless for active service. It was converted into a hulk and the engines were taken out and put into a new hull, which was also named the *Isabella Segunda*. This second man-of-war was wrecked off the Algerian coast in 1860.

The beautiful and sturdy sidewheeler *City of Monticello* was built in Wilmington, Delaware, in 1866. The ship's hull was 232 feet long, 32 feet wide and 11 feet deep and it was designed primarily for passenger traffic. In 1890, it was bought by a Canadian company and it travelled regularly between the large Canadian east coast ports until November 12, 1900.

The Charlottetown *Daily Patriot* reported on Monday, November 12, 1900: "In sight of the house tops of Yarmouth, the steamer *City of Monticello* foundered at sea Saturday morning." Thirty-three persons were drowned or dashed to death on the rock bound coast. Four perished in the furious storm that sent the old sidewheeler to the bottom.

The disaster occurred off Cranberry Head on the south side of Yarmouth Light within rifle shot of shore. The *Monticello*, battered by a gale that lashed the Bay of Fundy into a fury, sprang a leak. Frantic efforts were made to head the doomed vessel toward its home port, but it was held in the grip of the storm.

The life boats were quickly lowered and passengers and crew attempted to go ashore. One boat, with seven people on board, got away from the side of the *Monticello*, but it was nonetheless dashed to pieces in the surf. Only four occupants got safely to land. Two other boats that got away capsized in heavy seas and were battered on the rocks. Three minutes later, the *Monticello* swerved in the sea and sank.

All the next day, the bodies of the victims drifted ashore and, before nightfall, 24 had been recovered.

City of Monticello *foundering off Yarmouth, N.S., November 10, 1900. Yarmouth County Museum.*

City of Monticello, *Yarmouth County Museum.*

The *City of St. John,* was built in Carleton, now West Saint John, in 1870, for passenger traffic. It was 151 feet long with a 27-foot beam and ten-foot hold. On its first trip out of Saint John Harbour on May 26, 1870, it experienced boiler difficulties and was temporarily withdrawn from service. From then on, it ran to ports as far as the north shore of New Brunswick.

Mr. Enoch Lundt, the original owner, sold it to the Yarmouth Steamship Company in 1875. On July 30, 1875, the *City of St. John* was partially wrecked. It required extensive repairs and, in 1877, it was lengthened to 160 feet.

We next hear of the *St. John* when, on September 13, 1884, it was in Saint John Harbour and sold at auction to Captain George L. Burchell of Sidney, N.S., for $3,000. It was towed by the tug *Storm King* to Yarmouth, arriving May 31, 1885. There, at the Burrell and Johnson Yards, it was given a new boiler. Later the ship was sold to L. E. Baker and Captain Harvey Doane of Barrington who used it to run between Yarmouth and Halifax.

In 1902, after many years of service, this proud old wooden vessel was scrapped.

The *Fawn* was built at Carleton, N.B., and launched January 8, 1867. It was 179 feet long, had a 24-foot beam and an eight-foot draught. It was powered by a vertical beam engine with a 37-inch cylinder and a piston having an eight-foot stroke which developed 80 horsepower. The *Fawn* was the second of the "Floating River Palaces," along with the *David Weston,* built by Otis Small and Charles Hatheway who owned the Union Steamship Line. It ran from Saint John to Fredericton and Chipman, at the head of Grand Lake, for many years.

In 1877 the *Fawn*'s name was changed to the *Acadia*. In January, 1892, the *Acadia* burned in Saint John Harbour.

City of St. John, *1880. New Brunswick Museum.*

The Acadia. *New Brunswick Museum.*

Left:
Heather Belle, *Archives of Prince Edward Island.*

Right:
Marion, *New Brunswick Museum.*

The passenger steamer *Marion* was built in New York City in 1876. It was 142 feet long, 27 feet wide, and had an eight-foot draught. The *Marion* was used for local New York traffic until 1883 when it was sold to a Canadian company in Halifax. It ran along the east coast of Canada and the United States until it burned at Whycocomagh, N.S.

On October 31, 1922, the *Marion* was tied up at the wharf and the crew were getting ready to leave when the boat caught on fire. George Morrison stated that he thought that a spark or burning ember from the nearby tow boat had fallen into the engine room of the *Marion* which was open on the top. As soon as this spark got into the grease and oil, away went the fire. He was less than half a mile away and he saw the terrible blaze.

The wheelhouse was way up above the deck and, when it caught fire and fell, it blew the boat's whistle. The fire spread onto the wooden pier. People who were there, attempting to put out the fire, cut the lines holding the ship to the pier. Some of the crewmen had to jump off the second deck to get onto the wharf. There was a bit of a breeze and it carried the blazing hulk off. The *Marion* went aground, where its boiler remained for many years.

Three vessels were registered in Canada under the name *Heather Belle*. The first, built at Carleton, N.B., in 1861, burned at Fredericton in 1865.

The second was built in 1862 at Charlottetown. On April 19, 1864, *The Islander* newspaper reported that the *Heather Belle* had been hauled up on the Marine Railway and during the winter had undergone considerable improvement. The hull had been strengthened, the cabins enlarged and the ship completely repainted.

It kept a very busy schedule, leaving Charlottetown every Tuesday morning at four o'clock for Brush Wharf at Orwell. It would leave Orwell at 7:00 a.m. to return to Charlottetown, calling at Halliday's Wharf. Then back again it would go to Halliday's and Brush Wharf that evening, remaining overnight. This schedule was kept up Monday to Thursday. On Friday morning it left Charlottetown for Cranberry Wharf and East River at 4:00 a.m. and at 7:00 a.m.

Cabin fare was 30 cents, but on the trip to Crapaud, the cabin fare was 40 cents; 20 cents if you stayed on deck.

The second *Heather Belle* continued on its regular route until it was scrapped on October 1, 1883.

The third, the *Heather Belle*, shown in our photograph, was built at Mount Stewart, P.E.I., primarily to carry passengers, in 1883. It was 120 feet long, with a 34-foot beam and a seven-foot depth in the hold.

Very few paddle wheelers were used in Prince Edward Island because it lacked navigable rivers. The large centres were situated on the coast, exposed to the open sea, thus making sidewheelers and sternwheelers impractical.

There were three vessels registered in Canada under the name *Prince Rupert*. The ship in our photograph was built at Dumbarton, Scotland, by William Denny & Brothers, in 1894, as a passenger ship. It was 260 feet long, 32 feet wide and 12 feet deep, and weighed 1,158 gross tons.

The *Prince Rupert* sailed across the ocean to the Bay of Fundy and on August 5, 1895, the Halifax *Herald* tells of the marvellous new vessel, one of the fastest boats in the North American waters, a floating palace:

"Its engines developed 3,000 horsepower and enabled it to fly along in all weather and through any sea at a speed of 22 miles an hour." Unfortunately on the second day of its first trip, a high pressure cylinder gave out and it ran with one broken cylinder, which limited its speed to 16 miles an hour.

The engines were direct acting, triple expansion engines. There were eight corrugated furnaces to heat the boilers. Each engine had three cylinders, and their piston rods were of Siemens Martin Steel. There was an improved evaporating system, adequate to supply the ship's crew with fresh water for a voyage around the world. On no vessel were more majestic paddle wheels to be found, and when they revolved at full speed, it was said that it took a man with second sight to see the blades. The wheels had feathering paddles.

From a panel in the upper engine room, a flick of the wrist controlled an intricate and exquisite system of electric lighting. The ship was fitted throughout with 216 electric lights and the staterooms also had candles in electroplated sockets. There was a steam-heating apparatus in every corner of the vessel, allowing the passengers to regulate the temperature of their own staterooms.

The *Prince Rupert* had accommodation for 850 passengers. Two dining halls were decorated and upholstered in the most sumptuous fashion of the day. The woodwork was of specially-chosen white sycamore, the roof panelled in eucalyptus. The pillars shone like polished gold. The berths were pullman berths, and the staterooms could be converted in a few seconds into spacious drawing rooms, similar to a private section of a pullman parlour car, with cream and gold decorations, corduroy upholstery and silvered metal fittings. The ladies had a splendid bathroom with a mosaic floor and curtains of imbertine tapestry. The deck saloon, the latest in drawing room luxury, with its velour-panelled walls, square windows hung with silk tapestry, and electric fittings, was also reserved for the ladies.

The accommodations for gentlemen were modeled on exactly the same lines—the best. The smoking room was larger than one would find on most Atlantic liners, the walls had panels of leather, studded with brass. The upholstery, generally, was green buffalo hide. The square windows could be shaded with jalousie blinds. The gentlemen's bathroom had a supply of hot and cold water and salt water for showers.

"The *Rupert* makes two trips a day between Saint John and Digby, providing the quickest route between Halifax and Saint John and also affords the people of the city the quickest route to Boston by way of Yarmouth. Meals are served on board and it is a great pleasure to a traveller to take his time at supper in the

gorgeously furnished dining room.''

"The Captain, John Richards, is one of the most genial gentlemen you could desire to meet. He states, 'My business is to make my passengers comfortable and happy.' ''

The Saint John *Daily Telegraph*, September 27, 1904, gives us an idea of the kinds of problems these luxury boats encountered.

"The *Prince Rupert* did not arrive at its usual hour. However, about 2:30 p.m. the next day, news of the *Prince Rupert* had arrived from Digby. When it was thirteen minutes out from Point Prim Lights, a connecting rod pin bolt broke and this caused a second bolt to bend and thus, the steamer was disabled. The broken pin had to be bored out and it was 8:45 p.m. before the damage was repaired and

Prince Rupert, *Saint John Harbour. Public Archives of Canada, PA 20647.*

the *Rupert* was once more under full speed and headed for Saint John. The *Rupert* sailed for Digby at the usual hour the next morning and the damage was not serious.''

This fast, powerful ship continued to travel this route until 1913 when it was sold for service in the West Indies.

The *David Weston*, an early side paddlewheeler on the Saint John River, was built at Carleton, N.B., in 1866. Its hull was 177 feet long, 28 feet wide, eight feet deep.

It was built as the first of the "Floating River Palaces" by the newly-formed Union Steamship Line, the successor of the Hatheway & Small Steamship Line, after Fred Hatheway had died in 1866 and a new partnership was formed by his brother.

The *David Weston* was considered for the next thirty-seven years to be the best paddle-boat in design and sturdiness as well as in beauty. It had one of the longest and most useful careers of any Saint John steamer, travelling from Saint John to Washademoak Lake. It also made the Saint John, Fredericton run alternately with the *Acadia*.

"Three lives were lost and many people were injured in the burning of the Star Line steamer *David Weston* at Craig's Point about fifteen miles up river Saturday afternoon on her regular downward trip.''

The *Daily Telegraph* of Saint John, September 23, 1903, told the following story: "Fire broke out in some bales of hay on the lower deck. Fanned by the wind and fed by the dry and oily woodwork, the flames spread with great rapidity and in a few minutes the steamer was all ablaze amidships.'' The forty passengers frantically fled through the flames which enveloped the vessel from bow to stern.

"Captain Day ordered her beached and she was run ashore promptly. The three people who lost their lives were drowned, having jumped overboard from the burning vessel. They were: Etta Morrell of Indiantown, aged 21, a waitress; Fred Downey of Indiantown, aged 21, a deckhand; Stephen Rowan of Manchester, England, aged 11. He jumped overboard in fright from his aunt's arms and was drowned. His body is yet to be found.''

The David Weston *going downstream to Saint John at Cedars Wharf, King's County, New Brunswick, June 1899. Yarmouth County Museum.*

"The body of Miss Morrell, after being viewed by Captain Day, and the coroner, at Day's Landing, was brought to the City Saturday. The body of Fred Downey was found yesterday and brought to the saddened home of his people on Douglas Avenue. Of the forty-odd passengers, fully one-tenth have received injuries of greater or lesser extent and all are suffering from the shock of the tragedy which will rank as one of the most thrilling in the history of the province."

To some of the passengers, in their excitement there seemed to be only two choices: leaping overboard or burning. And to many, as they mounted the rail of the saloon deck, which was already on fire, and looked through 20 smoky feet of space to the water below, it seemed as though they were jumping into eternity. They leaped through a blinding world of cinders, sparks and smoke, only to fall into no more than three feet of water, with the bottom strewn with jagged rocks. Parents, almost overcome by the knowledge that their children were in some other part of the boat, literally fought their way through the fire to find them.

Practically all the survivors told the same tale: a sudden cry of fire; a gust of smoke; an orange gleam down amongst the bales of hay on the main deck; panic among the passengers, and the cool assurances of their safety by the captain and the crew.

The *May Queen* was built in 1869 at Carleton, N.B., by Otis Small and Charles H. Hatheway for the Union Steamship Line. It was 502 gross tons, 160 feet long, 25 feet wide, eight feet deep. The vertical beam engine had previously been used in the sidewheeler *Forest Queen*. The *May Queen's* usual run was on the Saint John and Salmon rivers.

It was first wrecked in a severe storm on Saturday, September 26, 1904, at Bailey's Point in Grand Lake. Captain Weston was the master. With over a hundred passengers and a large cargo aboard, he had left Newcastle and was heading for Chipman.

Page 8 of the Saint John *Daily Telegraph*, September 27, 1904, contained the following story:

"The *May Queen* is fast ashore. The oldest boat upon the river, the *May Queen*, grounded about five o'clock this Saturday afternoon at Bailey's Point, Grand Lake. She is not being refloated. She struck bottom in six feet of water and filled in about two hours. Her hundred passengers were landed in safety and the freight that was not damaged was promptly removed.

"The exact extent of the damage done to the boat is not yet known but it is feared that there is a big hole in the hull. Today men and appliances will be sent up for the purpose of endeavouring to raise her."

When the *May Queen* went aground, a heavy gale was blowing. For some reason, Captain Brennan, the former commander of the boat

The steamer May Queen *perhaps on the Saint John River, at a typical crude local dock. The water is shallow, although the minimum depth for this boat would be three feet. The passengers and crew have gathered on deck to have their pictures taken. New Brunswick Museum.*

who had navigated the river for some 40 years before retiring, was steering. The boat had been run 60 feet *inside* the buoy which indicated the shallows, and the shore was only a small distance away. When it became known that the steamer was on hard bottom, there was not much alarm among the passengers who were returning from an exhibition at Saint John. The boats were lowered and those aboard were quickly transferred to the beach.

The *May Queen* was valued at $15,000 and had $9,000 fire insurance but no marine insurance. It had been extensively repaired the previous spring.

In 1907-8 the *May Queen* was rebuilt, having new boilers installed and machinery rebuilt at a cost of $10,000. It was estimated that to build the same steamer at that time would have cost $90,000. The *May Queen* returned to its regular route.

Then, on February 2, 1918, it burned to the water's edge. Again the *Daily Telegraph* told the story: ''Steamer *May Queen* has burned.''

''The steamer *May Queen*, which had been in service on the Saint John River since the summer of 1869, early yesterday morning burned to the water's edge and sunk while at her moorings just below Milford on the western side of the Saint John River. The steamer was valued at $50,000 and was owned by the Grand Lake Steamship Company.

''The fire started early yesterday morning. When the day broke, all that was visible of her was the smoke stack and part of the boiler. After making her final trip last fall, she was moored for the winter at the old Cushing Mill Wharf.

''There was no fire in her boiler and none in her furnace. . . .''

The steamer had always been considered a lucky boat. It had sailed the waters of the Saint John for 48 years and during that time was ashore twice, but never damaged to an extent preventing it from making a trip. It was the fastest steamer on the river in the early decades of the century.

The *Star* was built in 1873 at the village of Portland, which is now part of Saint John. It was not registered with the Dominion of Canada, but in Saint John. The *Star* was 416 gross tons, 125 feet long, 23 feet wide and six feet deep.

The first owner was Mathias Hanson of Indiantown, which is now part of Saint John. In 1880, a Captain Vanmart sold it to the Union Steamship Line and for a while it belonged to the People's Steamship Line which was part of J. W. McLary & Company. For many years it was in the charge of Captain J. E. Porter on the Washademoak Lake run. It left Indiantown at 10:00 a.m. every Saturday, Tuesday, and Thursday and returned at 1:00 p.m. on Monday, Wednesday and Friday. It advertised a special one day trip as far as Oak Point and return for 50 cents.

In 1902, a fire on the *Star* set the main street of Indiantown ablaze. The *Daily Sun,* of St. John's, Newfoundland, reported on September 25, 1902: *"A big fire, steamer Star a total wreck at Indiantown."*

"At 2:30 o'clock this morning, an alarm was sent in for a fire at the Indiantown wharves and it was followed almost instantly by a second alarm that brought out the bulk of the city force.

"The fire broke out on the steamer *Star* as she lay at her moorings and spread so rapidly over the vessel that Isaac Warden, three men and two women who were on the steamer at the time, had a narrow escape for their lives. It is understood that the blaze started near the furnace but from what causes is unknown at this writing.

"The steamer was cast off as soon as possible and floated out into the stream, a burning hulk. From the steamer, the blaze, fanned by the wind, spread to the wharf and burned the big warehouse with all its contents,

Star, *New Brunswick Museum.*

chiefly hay and potatoes. Naize and Sons Warehouse, Williamson's Machine Shop, and Glazier's were also consumed.

"The fire, at an early hour this morning, was burning down Bridge Street towards Milton Marble Cove but there is little in that direction on which to exert its force.

"At four o'clock, the steamer *Star* was floating about Indiantown Harbour, a mass of flames; every now and then a crash of falling timbers and beams was heard as they gave way and fell into the river. The steamer is a total loss and the sinking portion had to be towed to shallow water. The sparks from the *Star* fire set fire to Tapley's large coal and oil sheds and they were totally destroyed.

"The *Star* was picked up by Tapley's tug, the *Wee Laddie,* and towed out into the stream so that further spread of the fire might be prevented. About half-past four o'clock,

Halley's tug, the *W. H. Murray,* went out and got a line on the burning steamer with the intention of towing her to Sand Cove and there beaching her, as it was thought that the machinery and the lower woodwork might be saved.

"When just off Green Head, the tow line was burned through and the *Star* immediately sank in what is comparatively deep water."

The *Star* was valued at $13,000, and was a total loss.

The *Crystal Stream* was a sidewheeler, built at Bull's Ferry, New Jersey, in 1873, as the *Nelson P. Hopkins*. It was 132 feet long, 25 feet wide and had a draught of nine feet. It was purchased in New York in 1902 by the People's Steamship Line and was put on the Washademoak route from Saint John to Coles Island. It was valued at $22,500 at the time it burned in 1907 but was insured for only $12,000. Coles Island, the scene of the tragedy, is in the Washademoak River about 60 miles from Saint John.

The Saint John *Daily Telegraph* reported Saturday morning, June 22, 1907: *"Four Die in Crystal Stream Fire, Awful Tales by Survivors, Agonizing Scenes Prevail, People Perished, Mutilated, Dismembered Bodies Found, Fearful Surroundings."*

"One of the worst tragedies on the Saint John River in the history of that waterway occurred in the early hours of Thursday morning when the steamer *Crystal Stream* took fire at Coles Island from some cause as yet undetermined, and burned to the water's edge. In the fire were cremated four of her crew while all the others had remarkable escapes. Some of them carry serious burns which will mark them for life."

Not long after midnight, as the steamer lay at the wharf, those on board awoke to find the vessel in flames. For some, escape was cut off, and, penned in a fiery furnace, they burned to death. Mrs. Chase, the stewardess, 71 years of age, found safety in a way almost incredible for one of her years. She climbed over the railing of the upper deck, her frail form lighted by the flames, billows of smoke rolling about her. She hung for a moment, and, in fear of the drop on one side but in greater fear of the fire above, let go and fell into a small boat which had been rowed out from the shore.

The mate, Herbert McCleery, and four

Built in 1905 at Hampton, N.B., the *Hampton* was 100 feet long, 21 feet wide, and had a five-foot draught. It carried up to 300 passengers on Kennebecasis Bay to Hampton until 1916, making a dozen stops along the way. Dinner was served for 35 cents, supper 30 cents, and a return ticket cost 60 cents.

The *Hampton* was owned by Harold Mabee of the Kennebecasis Steamship Company until 1917, when it was sold to the Fraser, James Gregory interests. It was continued on the same run until it was again sold, in 1917, this

The Hampton *towing a log boom near Saint John. Public Archives of Canada, PA 41726.*

time to the Majestic Steamship Company. Captain Dykeman ran it from Saint John to Belle Isle Bay. Gertude Porter bought it, January 31, 1924. After passing through the hands of the Eastern Canada Coastal S.S. Company, it was taken out of service in 1930. The last sternwheeler on the Saint John River, it was scuttled in deep water off Green Head.

men of the crew sleeping below deck, were aroused. The flames had made great headway, and every avenue of escape was cut off save one: a stairway to a trap door leading to the ladies' cabin. The trap door was closed and secured by the carpet which was tacked to the floor above. Over that, a stove had been placed. Rushing up the stairs to the trap door and calling to his half-wakened companions to follow, McCleery managed to force open the trap door. In his frantic efforts to tear away the carpet he overturned the stove setting fire to the cabin. Still, he was far from out of danger. To reach the outer air, he broke a window with his bare hands and made a dive for the water.

There was no sign of his four companions. They could not find the stairway in the blinding smoke and perished on the lower deck, while McCleery lay on shore bleeding fearfully from wounds made by the broken glass.

The loss included the total destruction of the *Crystal Stream,* as well as the long covered bridge between Coles Island and the mainland. There was also some damage to the island wharf. Rumour had it that there was a large amount of hay in the cargo deck and that there was no night watchman—a common practice.

The steamer *Aberdeen,* which narrowly escaped sharing the same fate as it lay so near the burning steamer, brought several of the survivors to Saint John the next day.

A large and anxious crowd was waiting. A horse-drawn ambulance was on hand to convey the seriously injured to the hospital and a coach waited to take the others home. When the gangplank was thrown out, there was a rush to get on board.

"Captain Perry of the *Aberdeen,* of which the *Crystal Steam* was a rival, said that his steamer lay at Coles Island near the *Crystal Stream* but

close to the beach. He thinks that Mrs. Perry was the first one on the *Aberdeen* to know of the fire, being awakened by the noise. She awakened him and he hurried ashore. By this time, the two women from the burning steamer had reached the wharf, and some of the others had landed, but nothing could be done for those who had been unable to leave. The *Aberdeen* was pulled to a place of safety while steam was quickly raised in its boilers to assist at the pumps and to help take it [the *Crystal Stream*] away from the burning dock.

"Surrounded by friends and relatives at her home, Mrs. Chase was seen by the *Telegraph* reporter soon after her arrival on the steamship *Aberdeen.* Mrs. Chase willingly answered all questions, although her burns must have been very painful. At times, she shook with sobs at the recollection of the terrible experience she had undergone and the horrible fate of the four young men of the crew. During the interview, several of Mrs. Chase's friends called and spoke feelingly of her misfortune."

Mrs. Chase said her room was on the second deck, opening into the saloon, a room which, with its organ and various articles of furniture, was used as a sitting room for the passengers.

The Crystal Stream. *Author's Private Collection.*

The sitting room opened onto the port side, which was the farthest from the wharf at that time, and so, she was at the greatest possible distance from the landing. The rest of the crew were in bed. The deck below was filled with hay, potatoes, and other produce destined for Saint John.

Mrs. Chase recalled, "I had a premonition that the fire was going to take place and said to myself, this is just the time for a fire. I thought of asking the cook to sit up with me but then I didn't like to ask as she would have thought it foolish. I decided, however, not to go asleep and about eleven o'clock I got up and dressed. This was only a half an hour before the outbreak.

"I lay down and slept and was awakened by someone screaming and recognized it as the voice of the cook who was calling out, 'Get up, the boat is on fire!' I jumped up," said Mrs. Chase, "and could see a bright light everywhere. It was about one o'clock and the light was so sharp you could pick up a pin from the floor."

As she stepped out into the saloon, she saw an impenetrable barrier of smoke and flames before her. She had taken off some of her clothing and thrown a macintosh over her head. On second thought, she made once more for the door and plunged into the smoke and flames, crying loudly that the boat was on fire and calling for help. Half-suffocated, she made her way to the door of the saloon and out into the passageway into the purer air. But even then, her position was precarious. The whole top of the vessel was burning and smoke was issuing from every crack and crevice. "I made for the railing. I saw a boat coming out and I don't know how I jumped from the rail but I did."

The purser, Mr. Bellyea, made a miraculous escape. His injuries were surprisingly minor. His face was blistered and scorched, his right hand and fingers were a mass of burnt flesh. But remarkable as it may seem, Mr. Bellyea's mustache and eyebrows were not even singed, despite the fact that the skin around them was cruelly burned.

Mr. Bellyea's room was situated near the paddle box on the side facing the waterfront. He was asleep at the time. He was awakened by the shrill screams of the women to find his room full of smoke and flames eating in on every side. He had been sleeping in his underclothes. He jumped out of bed, shoved his feet into the first pair of boots at hand, grabbed his coat, which had $70 of the company's money on the inside pocket, his vest and trousers, and made for the door, holding these items in his hands.

Losing his head, instead of taking the nearby door to the outer deck, he plunged into the very centre of the fire.

"The fire, he said, "was around the smoke-stack situated near my room. The heavy smoke choked while the glare of the fire blinded me.

I staggered forward and I got up to where the tables are. I fell from exhaustion, but the fall seemed to have benefitted me, for near the floor the smoke was less thick. I dropped my bundle and crawled forward along the floor, pushing an open door at the head of the saloon and out onto the deck. From there I climbed to the shore."

"Mr. Bellyea stated that the boat was loaded with hay from the engine room aft while there was none in the forward part. The fire, he feels, started amidships around the smoke-stack as it was near this portion that the heat was the most intense." A lantern always hung there and reporters suggested this might have exploded and set the hay on fire.

Mr. Bellyea stated that there was no watch-man on board as the crew usually sat up until about ten o'clock, and also that the women crew members were continually expressing their fear of fires.

The *Crystal Stream* kept rising out of the water as the weight of the top works lessened as they burned. Finally, they crashed over-board. The hulk swung around, blazing fiercely, and struck up against the Coles Island Bridge, setting it on fire and totally destroying it. The vessel went down with a hissing of steam and lay in about seven feet of water on an even keel between the wharf and the bridge, so that one could step from the wharf onto the wreck.

"The bodies of the four deck men were recovered but in such a charred state that they were no longer recognizable. The only one who could be in any way identified was one of the Logan boys."

Four ships were registered in Canada under the name *Aberdeen*. The *Aberdeen* in our photograph was registered in Saint John in 1894. It was 140 feet long, 22 wide and four feet deep.

It was originally called the *Florenceville*, built in 1879 by the York and Carleton Steamship Company. They ran it up the Saint John River under Captain Thomas Duncan as far as the country village of Florenceville. A stern-wheeler, it was designed with a wide flat bow for landing on the banks of the river as there were no wharves above Fredericton at this time. However, over the years, the level of the river seemed to go down and the vessel could no longer reach Florenceville; it was switched to the Fredericton, Woodstock route.

In 1894, it was sold to the Star Steamship Company which renamed it the *Aberdeen*, made many improvements, and ran it on the same route.

The *Aberdeen* carried freight and passengers. It cost 25 cents to transport a hogshead of molasses from Fredericton to Woodstock. Unlike many other boats of that time, the *Aberdeen* had three female members among its crew to cook and serve meals. Between trips, the boat would be used for moonlight excursions on the Saint John River. In 1894, it carried the material for the first telephone line from Woodstock, N.B. to Maine, up river.

On one part of the River, at Shogomac, the current is extremely swift, and the engineer, in order to navigate safely the fast waters, had to build up steam pressure in the boiler to over 100 pounds. This pressure was well over the safe legal limit and, to attain it, the safety valve had to be weighted down.

One of the last remaining members of the *Aberdeen*'s crew, Mr. John Woodman of Temperancevale, York County, N.B., told the Saint John *Telegraph Journal* in 1967, among other things, that the crew members worked for a dollar a day with meals and lodging included — good money in those days!

On June 16, 1908, the *Aberdeen* docked at Cody's Wharf on Coles Island at the usual time. All on board retired before ten o'clock with the exception of Captain Perry. They slept soundly until awakened by the alarm. At 1:20 a.m. mate Northrup and engineer Hutchison were awakened by the shouts of those on shore. They ran out and located the fire in the forward part of the ship. One look, and they knew the steamer was doomed. They quickly roused the sleeping members of the crew.

It was only the work of a moment for all hands to step ashore, but it was noticed that a Mrs. McLeod had failed to come. The alarm was sounded and Hutchison, who had been endeavouring to save his tools, ran out on the paddle wheel guard with the object of climbing up to help the woman. She appeared, however, and jumped down to the dock.

By this time, the lower part of the hull was so full of water that the steamer could not be entered and none of the crew could save their clothes. A large number of young men and women returning home after a dance watched the fire, and the men were called upon to assist in saving the village from a conflagration. They formed a bucket brigade. Water was poured onto the millhouse roof and the store. Further down the street, the cheese factory took fire but was extinguished by dint of hard work.

The crew of a nearby boat, the *Sincenness,* awakened by their night watchmen, had the time of their lives in saving the handsome rival of the *Aberdeen* from destruction. When the fire broke out, a light northwest wind had been blowing toward the *Sincenness* from the *Aberdeen.* Some of the crew turned on the hand pump, while others cast the *Aberdeen* off. A boat was lowered from the *Sincenness* to take

a line attached to the *Aberdeen* across the river. The burning hulk was then towed across and tied to the dome of the sunken *Crystal Stream* which was still sticking out of the water.

The sailors fruitlessly attempted to put out the fire. If there had been a strong wind blowing, nothing could have saved the *Sincenness.* However, in less than an hour, the fire burned itself out, and the *Aberdeen* settled on the bottom and lay partly submerged.

Those on board said that when it was discovered, the fire was forward of the boiler and the wood fuel, and was burning fiercely. A young man, who saw the fire from his room in the west boarding house on the wharf, said, "The fire was coming through the deck a little forward of the smokestack." All those on board said no hay was carried, that there were no lamps forward, and they also claimed that

all fires on board had gone out.

The engineer, Hutchison, stated that his fires were out by seven o'clock the night before when they tied up. "I was awakened by shouts on shore and ran out to find the steamer full of smoke. I left without any of my clothes. I found my way forward to the boiler. I came back, awakened the mate and the cook, and I got into my working clothes. I carried my tool chest ashore and was returning for more tools when someone cried, 'Mrs. McLeod is still on board.' She came out on the upper deck in what looked to be a dangerous place. I saw her climb over the rail and heard her say that she would be all right. She was just as cool as I am now. She told the mate not to bother laying a plank for her to walk ashore as she could easily leap the distance. By two o'clock it was all over."

Previous Page:
The Aberdeen, *The New Brunswick Museum.*

Victoria, *The New Brunswick Museum.*

The *Victoria* was built in 1897 at the Carleton Yards at Courtenay Bay in West Saint John, by Edward McGuiggan Jr. It was ordered by the Star Steamship Line at a cost of $57,000. Built of clear pine, its hull was 191 feet long, 30 feet wide and seven feet deep. The width at the paddle wheel covers was 55 feet; and the paddle wheels were 26 feet in diameter. The engine was taken from the American steamer *St. Lawrence,* which had sought safety in Saint John Harbour during the American Civil War, and was rebuilt by James Flemming.

The *Victoria* was renowned as the largest and most luxurious boat that ever travelled on the Saint John River. The furnishings were solid mahogany and the dining salon was gold and white. Mirrors between the windows completed the stately effect.

The *Victoria* could carry 995 passengers at a speed of 17 miles per hour, a speed which was attained on its first trip, September 17, 1897.

It was so fast that it could make the run from Saint John to McAlpine's Wharf, which is half way to Fredericton, in two hours and 29 minutes.

The *Victoria* was the only boat travelling from Saint John to Fredericton after the *David Weston* burned in 1903 and until the Star Line bought the *Majestic.* It was bought in 1911 by the Saint John River Steamship Company, and then, in 1913, by the Victoria Steamship Company. The *Victoria* retired from service in the fall of 1915 and burned at the Indiantown Wharf on February 3, 1916.

The Saint John *Daily Telegraph* told the story February 5, 1916: *"The steamer Victoria, which has plied the river between this city, Saint John, and Fredericton for the last nineteen years, was burned to the water's edge yesterday morning."*

The *Victoria* had been moored at Woodman's Point opposite Indiantown at the closing of navigation. There had been no history of fires on the ship and the origin of the blaze was a mystery. At about 4:00 a.m., a CPR engineer saw the streamer wrapped in flames. He blew his engine whistle to alert the residents of Farville.

An alarm was sounded but it was impossible for the firemen to get their engine to the wharf. Nothing could be done. Some went to the scene but the terrific heat drove them back. Unable to get any water, they stood helplessly by while the fire burned itself out. All that remained of the huge steamer was its engines, which sank alongside the wharf. Only the smokestack and some bent steel could been seen above the water line.

The St. Lawrence and the Saguenay

The early explorers of Canada could not sail their ocean-going craft up the St. Lawrence River because of the Lachine Rapids. Consequently they explored the Ottawa River, the St. Lawrence and Lake Ontario by canoe. Boats using the river route into the interior could go as far as Niagara, where they were obliged to portage around the rapids, or they could travel via the Ottawa River to Georgian Bay. The rest of the route was over the dangerous open waters of the Great Lakes.

The Great Lakes extend for 2,384 miles from the mouth of the St. Lawrence River at Belle Isle to Fort William at the head of Lake Superior. Early missionaries navigated Lake Superior by canoe in 1641. The era of larger vessels began in May of 1679. The *Griffon*, weighing ten tons, was built and launched at Cayuga Creek, a few miles above Niagara Falls. It disappeared mysteriously on its return voyage.

The first European traders on the St. Lawrence came in ocean vessels or freight canoes. As the population along the river increased and commerce grew, a different boat was needed: one which could carry bulk cargo through shallow waters. Nineteenth century sailors borrowed the design of a European boat, commonly seen in French and western English channel ports. It was essentially a barge, called by its Québécois adaptors the "pinflat".

The rigging and sail on this boat was known as the "Polacca Rig"; a wide, squared sail ran on the lower course and its feeder ends were fastened to a heavy yardarm extending from the lower mast just above the deck. Pinflats carried heavy freight such as lead, iron, bricks and lumber from Lower Canada to the sparse settlements on Lake Ontario.

As the freight increased, the rivermen began building "bateaux." These were large flat-bottomed skiffs, sharp at both ends, forty feet long and six feet deep. They drew about twenty inches of water and their thick bottoms were not easily damaged by rocks. They were provided with several sets of oars, pushing poles, and a steering oar. They had masts fifteen feet high which supported a square lugsail.

These boats could carry from three to five tons, or about thirty-five barrels of flour. At this time barrels were the packing containers of choice. Eggs were packed in sawdust-filled barrels; liquids transported in barrels of from five to fifty gallons.

After a few years, American traders from the Mohawk Valley introduced the superior Durham boats into the river traffic. These were long, relatively light and had a shallow draught. The bottoms, not as flat as those of the bateaux, were made of white oak, and the sides, which were less vertical, of pine. Durham boats had eight to ten times the capacity of the more cumbersome bateaux.

The earliest Canadian shipyard was on the banks of the River St. Charles in Québec. From 1732 on, it built ships for export to France. The shipbuilders of Québec under the French régime were pioneers in the construction of large sailing vessels. Perhaps it was this tradition which lead to their later achievement in building steamboats.

The first paddlewheeler to be built in the province was the *Accommodation*, which ran between Québec and Montréal in 1809. This boat was requisitioned to carry British troops for the War of 1812. The *Lauzon* took over its route from 1817 on.

Typical of steamboats on the St. Lawrence was the *Queenston*, of 1824. It was constructed with an English steeple-type engine, even though the American designed walking beam engine had been popular for several years. The single "main" or "power" cylinder of the *Queenston* was fifty-six inches in diameter, with a stroke of ten feet. It received steam from two box-type square marine boilers which burned nothing but hardwood.

By 1840 the construction of wooden steamships and engines had changed radically. Experience now enabled engineers to build vessels double their previous length. The longitudinal, sponson-type paddlewheel guards had proved themselves seaworthy and practical, even in rough open water. Fore-and-aft rigidity of the longer vessels was attained with arch-type trusses along the hull; the *Ploughboy* is an excellent example of this.

In 1845, the world's largest inland transportation company began in the small village of St. Charles on the Richelieu River. It was

Previous Page:
The sidewheeler Queen *was built at Sorel in 1840 by David Vauthan, 206 feet long and 26 feet wide. In 1843 the ship was lengthened to 235 feet and sold to the St. Lawrence Steamboat Company. At that time the Company was owned and run by John Molson, the founder of Molson's Brewery and Molson's Bank (later to become the Bank of Montreal).*

Molson attempted to start a steamboat service along the St. Lawrence River. The Accommodation *of 1809, his first ship, was unsuccessful because of its primitive technology. It was followed by the* Swiftsure *in 1812 and the* Malsham *in 1815. By 1816, a rival boat, the* Car of Commerce, *began operation. This prompted Molson to add two even more powerful boats, the* Lady Sherbrooke *and the* New Swiftsure. *Nonetheless, he ultimately gave up the line as unprofitable.*

The Queen *continued to run between Montréal and Québec City until it was scrapped in 1860. Metropolitan Toronto Library Board.*

started by farmers seeking an efficient means of getting their produce to the Montréal market. They raised £3,500 to build their first steamboat; the *Richelieu*. Their new society was called *La Société de Navigation de la Rivière Richelieu*, and the boat travelled twice a week between Chambly and Montréal.

In 1847 the society took on a new partner and changed its name to *La Compagnie de Richelieu*. There had been steam navigation for many years between Montréal and Québec City, but these enterprises were not always successful. When the *Compagnie* put on two handsome new steamers, the *Victoria* and the *Napoléon*, in August of 1856, it swept all competitors from the river. The same year saw the acquisition of the *Jacques Cartier*, the *Castor* and the *Cultivator*, all sidewheel steamboats.

A new company was now formed, the Montreal and Three Rivers Navigation Company. In 1861, it built the *Montréal;* in 1865, the *Québec* and in 1867, the *Canada*. All were sidewheelers. From then on the company acquired, or amalgamated with, all the small, local steamboat lines operating in the vicinity of Montréal and the Saguenay River. The Saguenay, which flows south to the St. Lawrence below Québec City, is one of the most scenic rivers in the world. In many places, mountains over a thousand feet high rise abruptly from the water's edge. It is navigable for seventy-eight of its hundred-and-ten miles, to a point eight miles above Chicoutimi.

The Saguenay was a major highway for the shipment of pulp and paper to foreign markets, and the first steamboats on the River operated mainly as towboats for logbooms and barges. But the magnificent passenger steamers that travelled between Montréal and Québec City stopped at the holiday resort town of Tadoussac on the north-eastern shore of the River. The lodge was equipped with a large pier at which sidewheelers like the *Québec,* the *Pittsburgh* and the *Montréal* could dock.

It is interesting to note that, at this time, the passage from Montréal to Québec City was $1.50 first class, or $1.00 if one stayed on deck. When there was competition, the rates were cut to $1.00 for berth and meals and 75 cents for berth only.

In 1875, long years of negotiation ended with *La Compagnie de Richelieu* amalgamating with the Canadian Navigation Company (previously known as the Royal Mail Line) which ran from Toronto to Montréal. The Canadian Navigation Company was headed by Sir Hugh Allen of Canadian Pacific Railways fame.

The new company was known as the Richelieu and Ontario Navigation Company. It operated a formidable fleet of eighteen ships between Toronto and Québec City. In 1894, control passed into the hands of yet another group, headed by the Hon. L.J. Forget.

The first vessel to be built by the new owners was the *Toronto*. It was far ahead of anything afloat on Canadian waters and attracted a great deal of attention. Then came the *Kingston,* slightly larger, and the mighty *Montréal*. Later boats were screw propeller steamers; the *Rapids King,* the *Québec,* the *Rapids Prince* and the *Saguenay*. The Richelieu and Ontario continued its policy of expansion, and, in 1913, the Canada Steamship Lines were formed, providing service from the tip of Lake Superior down the St. Lawrence, and all the way to South America.

In the first half of the nineteenth century, the Québec shipbuilding industry prospered, like that of the Maritimes, because of a plentiful supply of cheap timber. Then, in 1843, the first iron steamers came into use on

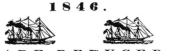

the St. Lawrence. They were ferryboats manufactured in Scotland but assembled in Canada, and travelled between La Prairie and St. Lambert. By about 1880, steel was favoured in the production of boat hulls. Québec had neither the technology nor the reserves of iron to compete with Scotland and the United States. It was not until after the First World War that the shipbuilding industry revived again.

The *Accommodation* was the first Canadian steamboat to travel the St. Lawrence River. It was ordered by the rich brewery family of John R. Molson, based in Montréal. Work on the hull was begun in March of 1809 by John Bruce; the boat was launched on August 9th. The engines were cast at the Forges St. Maurice, and the machining performed locally by Ezekial Cutler and George Platt.

The *Accommodation* was 85 feet long and 16 feet wide, with berths for twenty passengers. It was driven by a single cylinder steam engine which turned open, double-spoked side paddle wheels. It had a mast to which could be affixed a sail when the wind was reasonable. The boat did not have sufficient power to combat the heavy winds which occasionally blow across the St. Lawrence.

It left Montréal on its maiden voyage November 1, 1809 and arrived in the port of Québec on November 4th. The trip took a total of sixty-six hours, half of which was spent at anchor. Passage to Québec City on the *Accommodation* only cost $9.00, and the return fare to Montréal was $8.00

In 1810 the *Accommodation* only made ten trips, most of its time being spent on repairs and alterations to machinery. The plumbing was inadequate, and the engine simply too small.

During the War of 1812-14, the *Accommodation* carried British troops up the St. Lawrence from Québec City. Soon after, it was retired from service and scrapped.

Soon after, the *Accommodation* was retired to make way for more powerful ships.

The Accommodation, *Metropolitan Toronto Library Board.*

Kingston *on the Upper St. Lawrence River. Notman Collection, McCord Museum.*

The *Kingston* had one of the most unusual histories of any ship on the Great Lakes, all due to the great strength and durability of its iron hull. It was originally built in Montréal in 1855 by the Bartley and Dunbar Company. The hull was iron, 176 feet long, 27 feet wide, ten feet deep and weighed 345 tons. It had a vertical beam engine and paddle wheels 26 feet in diameter.

The design was rather unusual in that the vertical beam engine was located in the middle of the ship between the port and starboard boilers. Each boiler had a smokestack; the beam can be seen in our picture, between them. This permitted much more passenger space, but the engine room was very cramped.

In 1855, the *Kingston* was placed on the Montréal to Toronto route. On August 28, 1870, the Prince of Wales, later King Edward VII and at that time the Governor-General, boarded the *Kingston* at Dickinson's Landing, steamed down the St. Lawrence River, through the various rapids, and back to Montréal, arriving early in the evening. The Prince also rode on the *Kingston,* September 7, for a trip from Cobourg to Toronto, and on September 14, when it brought the royal party back to Montréal from Toronto.

On June 11, 1872, the *Kingston* left Brockville at 1:30 p.m. with about 100 passengers on board. Off Grenadier Island, 18 miles above Brockville, fire was discovered in one of the rooms near the smokestacks. Alarm was given but the fire spread with such rapidity that the *Kingston* was turned around, headed for Grenadier Island, and beached on the shore. Only one lifeboat could be launched. It capsized and a woman drowned. Another woman drowned when she jumped from the steamer into the water and her life preserver, being improperly adjusted, prevented her from swimming. The

Kingston burned to the water's edge, a complete wreck.

The hulk was salvaged and brought to the Kingston shipyard where it was rebuilt using the original engines. Renamed the *Bavarian* in 1872, it continued on the same route.

The Toronto *Globe,* Friday, November 7, 1873, read: *"Steamer Bavarian Burned, Fourteen Lives Lost."*

"Oshawa—The steamer *Bavarian* took fire last night about eight o'clock when sailing opposite Oshawa. She was a mass of flames in an instant and there was only time to load two lifeboats. They reached land containing twenty-two persons. There were fourteen people remaining, who are without a doubt lost. . ."

A survivor reported, "Among those lost was Captain Charles Carmichael of Toronto. There was very little screaming or anything of that sort, but when we were leaving the steamer, I heard something like a moaning. Someone said they saw two women standing on her

The Algerian, *Long Sault Rapids, St. Lawrence River, Ontario. Notman Collection, McCord Museum.*

stern. The last I saw of Captain Carmichael, he was in the water holding onto a plank. He called out 'Charlie' to the second mate and went over to him."

The burned-out iron hull was towed to Kingston where it was once again rebuilt as a passenger steamer of the same dimensions. In 1874, it was again launched and, as the *Algerian,* it ran from Toronto to Montréal for many years.

In 1904, the hull was once again given a new name: the *Cornwall.* In Kingston, in 1913, the hull was lengthened to 177 feet, although the beam remained at 27 feet and the depth at ten. The gross tonnage was increased to 588. This vessel was scrapped in 1930 at the Steel Company of Canada's Hamilton plant.

The *Napoléon* was built in Montréal in 1856. It was 168 feet long, 25 feet wide, and eight feet deep, and was given the registration number 274. It was built to carry passengers and freight, unlike its predecessor, *Napoléon III,* which was constructed in 1855 as a towing tug.

On June 26, 1857, the *Napoléon* sailed from Québec harbour. About 5:00 p.m., the Captain saw the steamer *Montréal* on fire in mid-river. The *Napoléon* raced to the rescue and took ten cabin and one hundred and nine steerage passengers on board. The *Montréal* had left Québec only a few hours earlier, carrying three hundred and thirty newly arrived Scottish immigrants. One hundred and fifty-seven lives were lost in this disaster.

The *Napoléon* continued its service between Montréal and Québec until it was scrapped in 1870.

The Chambly, *the* Napoléon, *the* Europa *and the* Terrebonne *in Montréal Harbour, c. 1865. Notman Collection, McCord Museum.*

There were six steamboats registered in Canada under the name *Montréal*. The vessel in our photograph was built by a Montréal shipyard in 1860, as a passenger boat. It was 262 feet long, 32 feet wide and nine feet deep. In 1886 it was sold to the St. Lawrence Steam Navigation Company, and ran between Montréal, Québec City and the Saguenay River ports.

In 1902 the ship was refitted, and named the *Beaupré*. It still retained its original hull number, 2211. As the *Beaupré* it continued to sail from Montréal until 1913, when the superstructure was removed and the hull was turned into a barge.

The Montréal *under way. Notman Collection, McCord Museum.*

The Montréal. *Notman Collection, McCord Museum.*

The Montréal, *an interior view, c. 1880. Ontario Archives.*

Fourteen boats were registered in Canada under the country's name. The *Canada* in our picture was built at Sorel in 1866. It was 248 feet long, 31 feet wide and 11 feet deep, and was driven by a single cylinder vertical beam engine. The *Canada* ran between Montréal, Québec City and Saguenay River ports.

In 1905 this ship was rebuilt at Sorel and enlarged to 268 feet long and 58 feet wide. Its new name was *St. Irenée*, but it resumed its former passenger run. Renamed the *Cape St. Francis* in 1920, it was laid up the following year. During most of its life, this ship was owned by the Canada Steamship Lines.

Notman Collection, McCord Museum.

St. Irenée, *Québec City Harbour. Notman Collection, McCord Museum.*

Dining Salon of Canada, *Notman Collection, McCord Museum.*

The Canada, *the smoking room. Notman Collection, McCord Museum.*

The *Virginia* was built as a passenger steamer at Wilmington, Delaware, in 1879. It was 251 feet long and 35 feet wide, and travelled to both American and Canadian seaports.

In 1903 the *Virginia* was registered as a Canadian ship. Two years later it ran aground off Crane Island in the lower St. Lawrence River, and sustained heavy damage. It was successfully refloated in a month, then repaired and renamed the *Tadoussac*. Under the latter designation, it continued its route on the St. Lawrence until it was scrapped in 1918. The name *Tadoussac* was given to an entirely different passenger steamer in 1928.

The Virginia, *later the* Tadoussac, *at Montréal. Notman Collection, McCord Museum.*

La Prairie *on the St. Lawrence River. Notman Collection, McCord Museum.*

The *La Prairie* was built in Montréal in 1867, with dimensions of 178 feet in length, 28 in width and nine in depth. It ran between Montréal, Québec, Tadoussac and La Prairie. Rebuilt at Sorel in 1894 to 198 feet long, the *La Prairie* continued as a passenger boat until it burned in the harbour of La Prairie on July 24, 1909.

The *Lady of the Lake* was built in Magog, Québec. It was constructed for carrying passengers, with dimensions of 153 feet long and 26 feet wide. This ship ran between St. Lawrence River ports until it was scrapped in 1917.

Lady of the Lake, *c. 1880, Notman Collection, McCord Museum.*

The *Berthier* was built in Sorel in 1870. It was 184 feet long, 29 feet wide and nine feet deep and was equipped as a passenger steamer.

The Montréal *Gazette*, May 25, 1914, reported: "In one of the most spectacular fires seen along the river front in years, the steamer *Berthier* of the Richelieu and Ontario Navigation Company burned and sank at her mooring alongside Victoria Pier last night, an hour after she had arrived here from Berthierville, Québec."

When the fire was first discovered by the engineer, the crew had time to get ashore two horses and a number of sheep. But they overlooked the cook and three other men who were in their berths. They were rescued by firemen.

"One of them, Mercier the cook, 64 years of age, had his hands so badly cut in breaking through a window to escape being burned to death that he had to be taken to the Nôtre Dame Hospital. Firemen slid along a hawser from the wharf to the stern of the steamer to catch Mercier, who was suffocating from the dense smoke. Then a short ladder was passed across to him by Deputy Chief Mann, on which Mercier and the three other men, who were rescued from the stern of the steamer, were able to reach the wharf.

"It is thought that the fire must have been burning somewhere between the decks before the *Berthier* reached her moorings. It broke out suddenly a short while after the passengers, who had come from Sorel, had gone ashore and it spread so rapidly that by the time the first fire fighters reached the scene, the steamer was ablaze on the two upper decks from stem to stern."

Deputy Chief Mann, and others, had lines of hoses laid from the hydrants on Commissioner Street. As the fire engines arrived, they were brought down to the edge of the wharf beside

the burning steamer. A dozen streams of water were pumped into the hull. The tugs *St. Peter* and *John Pratt* of the Harbour Commission worked their hoses from Victoria Basin.

Eventually the *Berthier* listed dangerously to starboard (because of the amount of water poured into her), and the tugs backed away to a safe distance. Soon the starboard rail was under water, with the port rail high above the wharf. As the *Berthier* slid off the edge of the wharf, it righted itself as if it might settle down gradually on an even keel. But it sank stern first and broke amidships when it touched bottom in 25 feet of water.

The mast fell as the steamer went down, but the wheelhouse remained intact. Lifeboats and chairs on the upper deck floated off into

The Berthier *in the St. Lawrence River. Public Archives of Canada.*

Victoria Basin. An electric bell in the wheelhouse kept ringing until one of the firemen smashed the connection with a blow of his axe.

Even after the steamer had gone down, Deputy Chief Mann had to keep pouring water upon the wreck to extinguish the flames which still burned in the wheelhouse and under the roof of the top deck. There were between 75 and 160 passengers on board, many of them women and children. All were saved.

Montréal Harbour, c. 1910, showing the Berthier *(right foreground). Notman Collection, McCord Museum.*

The sidewheeler *St. Lawrence* was originally 210 feet long, 28 feet wide, and 19 feet deep, and was built in New York City in 1852. It was bought by the St. Lawrence Steam Navigation Company, renamed, and used on the Saguenay River route. Its first port of call was Baie St. Paul where the harbour was so shallow the larger steamers could not enter. From there it went down the North Shore to Murray Bay and on to the Rivière du Loup for connection with the Intercolonial Railway. The next port was Tadoussac, and the cruise ended at St. Alphonse, now known as Bagotville.

Public Archives of Canada, PA 8746.

The *Bohemian* was built in Montréal in 1873, 175 feet long and 27 feet wide. It carried passengers from Montréal to other St. Lawrence River ports, and was owned by the Richelieu and Ontario Company.

The *Bohemian* was rebuilt at Sorel in 1900 to 195 feet in length. In 1905 it was renamed the *Prescott*, but continued its old route until August 27, 1909, when it burned in Montréal harbour.

The front page of the Montréal *Herald*, Saturday, August 28, 1909, carries the heading *"Steamer Prescott destroyed in a brilliant blaze, crowds throng the wharf at midnight to see it."*

With an estimated loss of $40,000, the steamer *Prescott*, of the Richelieu and Ontario Navigation Company, burned to the water's edge and sank in her berth off the Victoria pier after bringing a merry party of American delegates down the rapids only the day before.

The *Prescott* ran between Montréal and Prescott until driven out of business by the

The *Prescott running the Lachine Rapids, C. 1906. Notman Collection, McCord Museum.*

newer *Rapids King* and *Rapids Queen.* It had been taken out of commission that summer and offered for sale, being used in the meanwhile for occasional excursions. It had been moored to the pier the previous day to take on coal and was lying there until shortly after 10:00 p.m. when the fire started. As far as could be learned, it originated in the boiler room. In a few minutes, the ship was a mass of flames.

The fire fighting force from the city of Montréal arrived promptly under Chief Tremblay. Captain Joseph Seguin of the fire tug, *St. Peter,* also noticed the flames and immediately gave the order for full speed ahead. In three minutes, he had arrived with his powerful little tug and started his pumps, hosing down the inferno.

Nearby, the vessel *Trinidad,* under Captain Mackenzie, started its pumps. Three of its boilers were cold but in the fourth there was sufficient steam to operate three powerful pumps. The Captain used two lines of hose for the burning steamer; one he kept to hose down his own boat so that it would not catch fire.

In a few minutes, by 10:35 p.m., the steamer and a nearby storage shed were a roaring mass of flames. Bales of hay lying on the wharf 60 feet away had caught fire from the fierce heat, although protected by tarpaulins. The old steamer was afire from stem to stern, the shed invisible for smoke and flames, and only glimpses of firemen at work could be seen. The *St. Peter* was as close as she dared be and was pouring tons of water into the heart of the conflagration.

The *Prescott's* funnel had fallen long before and was draped all over the crushed side of the boat. It was red hot as far back as could be seen. Only the walking beams stood stiff and

majestic, apparently uninjured in the general ruin.

Some the hempen mooring lines of the *Prescott* caught fire and part of the vessel began to swing away from the pier into the open harbour. This endangered two other steamers lying at the end of the pier with their bows projecting right in the path of the burning derelict.

As the *Prescott* swung off to point into the channel, one of the several tugs which had stood by, at a very considerable risk, passed a chain cable aboard.

This tug, the *Dupré,* towed the two craft towards land again and the chain cable was eventually attached to the shore. At 11:35 p.m., when the flames had been beaten down,

Bohemian entering Lachine Canal. Notman Collection, McCord Museum.

the steamer *Virginian* sailed majestically up the river with Lord Charles Beresford aboard. He had an excellent view of the blazing steamer and an unusual welcome to her great city.

At 12:15 a.m., there were still five steamers playing their hoses on the burning hulk. The combination of the fire eating through the dry wooden hull and the tons of water thrown into her caused the boat to gradually settle deeper and deeper into the water until, at 1:25 a.m., it sank quietly into 35 feet of water. Only a few blackened timbers and fired, tortured pieces of steel mark her grave. The *Prescott* was fully covered by insurance.

The *Duchess of York* was built in Montréal in 1895 as a passenger steamer. 157 feet long and 25 feet wide, its service on the St. Lawrence and Ottawa rivers was the longest of any excursion ship.

In 1925 the vessel was rebuilt as the *Sorel* and in 1927 as the *Pelerin*. In 1934 the *Duchess* underwent its final metamorphosis, into the *Beloeil*. As the *Beloeil*, it took excursions on the Ottawa River between Carillon and Montréal.

Finally, in 1938, the superstructure of the old *Duchess of York* was removed, and its hull was used as a pulpwood barge.

Duchess of York *in the Lachine Rapids, c. 1910. Notman Collection, McCord Museum.*

*Pelerin in the harbour of Québec City, Notman
Collection, McCord Museum.*

The passenger steamer *Québec* was built in Lauzon, Québec, in 1928. It was 350 feet long and 70 feet wide, and one of three sister ships launched at the Davie shipyards that year. The other two boats were the *St. Lawrence* and the *Tadoussac*.

On June 19, 1930, the *Quebec* ran aground on the White Island Reef, in spite of the warning signals sent by an anchored lightship. It continued to sail, however, and in 1938 was adopted as a cruise ship by the Canada Steamship Lines. Its route on the Saguenay River ran from Bagotville to Montréal.

The *Globe and Mail,* Toronto, August 15, 1950, reported *"Four hundred and seventy-five Flee Blazing CSL ship on Saguenay Holiday Cruise."*

"The fire started at 5:10 p.m. when the cruiser was twenty minutes off Tadoussac. The crew was unable to control the blaze and the ship was ordered into dock at top speed. All passengers were off by 6:00 p.m. The ship was tied alongside a cement dock and the Tadoussac Fire Department helped fight the fire. At 9:30, the ship was expected to blow up—the fire neared the boiler room—but by 11:00 the blaze was under control.

"The fire had burned down to the freight deck which was on the same level as the passengers' dining room. The fire was believed to have started in the linen department, the same place as the fire which broke out on the *Noronic.* As the ship was docked, some passengers went over the side on ladders to the safety of the pier. Others went through on normal gangways. A few passengers and crew suffered light burns."

Reports from the scene said that the *Québec* arrived at the Tadoussac dock, with lifeboats ablaze and flames shooting from the decks. As it burned to the waterline, the decks collapsed, indicating what might have happened, had the

The steamer Québec *in Montréal Harbour, c. 1884. Notman Collection, McCord Museum.*

ship been a few miles further away from an accessible port when the fire broke out.

A survivor, Dr. H. F. Snevel, stated: "If there was a sprinkler system aboard this ship, we didn't see it working. . . . We hardly had time to dress and get out of our cabin. Even the shirt I am wearing is borrowed. We went down to our cabin after lunch to have a nap. Shortly afterwards we were awakened by people shouting, 'Put on your lifebelts.' Smoke poured into the cabin. . .

"We got up to put our lifebelts on and went

on deck. Everything seemed calm, except on A deck. Smoke was pouring out all over the place, people were standing around with their lifebelts on. Other were running around pouring water on the decks. No general alarm was sounded. We think the fire started on A deck and not on B deck. On A deck, things seemed to be in a panic. One old couple crawled into a lifeboat in order to get away from the smoke. They were severely affected before they were dragged out as they had pulled the tarpaulin over their heads.

"I broke a porthole window and managed to get some air. Then I tried to help her husband out, he was cut badly on the arm by broken glass. During that time, I lost my wife. I tried to go back in the cabin to find her but the passageway was half-filled with water by that time. Finally I found her on deck. Everyone was coughing with smoke. The ship was headed for Tadoussac: it took about a half an hour to get there, I think."

Dr. Snevel and his wife left their car in Montréal:"I'll get it and head home when my nerves are calmer."

The Montréal *Gazette*, Wednesday, August 16, had some further revelations: "The cruise ship *Québec*, which burned with a loss of

Smoking salon of the Québec. *Ontario Archives.*

Montage of the sidewheeler Québec *before the Citadel of Québec. Notman Collection, McCord Museum.*

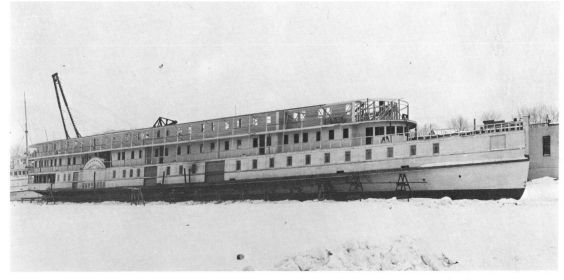

The construction of the superstructure of the steamer Québec. *Notman Collection, McCord Museum.*

at least three lives, was permitted to operate temporarily minus some of the improvements required under the new Federal Safety Regulations, it was learned today. The new regulations were framed after and as a direct result of the *Noronic* disaster at Toronto last year.

"Transport Department officials were extremely reluctant to discuss the matter and admitted some of the changes and improvements required in the law had been waived by the Transport Departments until the end of the present cruise season. They declined to state the nature of the improvements which were waived, but they said that, to the best of their knowledge, they [the improvements] were minor modifications which had no bearing on the present shipping tragedy.

"A sprinkler system had been installed and it had fire resistant bulkheads as a result of the terrible lessons learned in the *Noronic*. Other changes required by the regulations had been in progress while the cruise season was in full swing."

By August 18, the number of victims had risen to seven, and two passengers, Gertrude and Eva Toub of Terrytown, New York, were still missing.

The company was unable to pin down with certainty the exact number of passengers. A list of passengers with cabins, the only list, was destroyed in the fire.

The Ottawa

The Ottawa River System was once the main highway into the interior of North America; "La Grande Rivière du Nord." Until the completion of the Canadian road and railway lines around 1900, travellers stayed on the rivers to go long distances, and avoided the exposed, rough waters of the Great Lakes. Most early voyagers travelled in small boats or canoes which would be helpless in storms on the Great Lakes but which were quite safe on sheltered rivers. A further advantage of the rivers was that game could easily be hunted along their banks.

The Ottawa River is the greatest tributary of the St. Lawrence, and it is still the shortest water route west to the Great Lakes. The typical route inland began at the north shore of the St. Lawrence River and proceeded to the mouth of the Ottawa near Lachine. (So called because of the delusion of the first explorers that they were headed for the Orient.) One then travelled north-west to the Carillon Rapids, which had to be portaged, then rejoined the River where the town of Grenville now stands. It was possible to continue up the Ottawa River to the Mattawa, and thence into Lake Nipissing. Canoes usually stayed on the south shore of the Lake and then went westward along French River to Georgian Bay. From there one could continue north into Hudson's Bay, west to Lake Superior and the Prairie Provinces, or south-west to Lake Michigan and eventually down the Mississippi River into the central United States.

The Hudson's Bay Company used the Ottawa River System to send and receive all of its trade goods to the Canadian west and north. Fur traders and lumberjacks relied on the river route to transport their goods; in fact lumber traffic was for many years the major activity on the Ottawa. After the War of 1812, maintenance of the Ottawa canals was considered vital to the defense of British North America. And with the establishment of the city of Ottawa as the new Dominion's capital in 1867, passenger and freight ships between Ottawa and Montréal multiplied enormously. Businessmen and politicians now had to travel frequently between Montréal, the economic capital of Canada, and Ottawa, the political capital.

The navigability of the Ottawa River is interrupted by rapids between the villages of Carillon and Grenville, but in 1834, the first Carillon Canal was finished. It allowed small boats to bypass the rapids without a portage. It was built by soldiers as a possible alternate route to Fort York should the Americans close the St. Lawrence River access.

The Ottawa River saw its first steamboat in 1822. This ran between Grenville (above the rapids) and Ottawa. Increasing river traffic lead to the formation of the first company to engage in transport on the Ottawa River, the Ottawa and Rideau Forwarding Company, in 1830. The company ran boats above and below the rapids at Carillon, with a connecting coach system between Carillon and Grenville.

In 1842 the Ottawa Steamer Company was organized to provide integrated transport between Montréal and Ottawa. By 1851 the numerous rapids in the St. Lawrence River were bypassed by canals and it was possible to carry heavy freight from Montréal to Toronto directly, instead of by the slower route along the Ottawa via the Rideau Canal and Kingston.

By 1860, the Ottawa Steamer Company was running a regular daily schedule between Ottawa and Montréal, and small passenger steamers travelled the upper Ottawa River as far as Mattawa. In 1864, the company changed its name to the Ottawa River Navigation Company. It continued to provide an integrated daily service both ways between Montréal and Ottawa. The boats from Ottawa stopped at Grenville, the passengers taking a coach or railway around the Carillon rapids to Carillon where they reembarked and continued to Montréal. Those coming from Montréal got off at Carillon and reembarked at Grenville.

In 1907 the railway ran along the banks of the Ottawa. It could guarantee all-weather service, and the steamboats were unable to compete with it. The Ottawa River Nagivation Company was sold to the Central Railway of Canada, and the steamers gradually disappeared from the Ottawa River.

The *Queen Victoria* was built in Hull, Québec, by A. Cantin of Montréal. The steamer was 170 feet long, 23 feet wide, and had a seven-foot draught. It weighed 651 tons. Its paddle-wheels were 28 feet in diameter. Cantin delivered it to the Ottawa Steamer Company on July 15, 1861.

The *Queen Victoria* ran on the Ottawa River between Ottawa and Grenville, Québec, until 1873 when the *Peerless* replaced it, and the *Queen Victoria* became the night boat. Passengers for Montréal would disembark at Grenville and take the Carillon and Grenville Railway the 13 miles to Carillon where they would board the *Princess* for the remainder of the run.

In 1881, the Montréal, Ottawa and Occidental Railway began operating on the north shore of the Ottawa River between Ottawa and Montréal and the boat lines lost their passenger traffic. The *Queen Victoria* was sold to the Victoria Park Transportation Company of Toronto. The new owners found to their dismay that it was too large for the Carillon and Grenville Canal which bypasses the Long Sault Rapids in the Ottawa River. They waited until spring, for high water, and floated it over the rapids. It was the largest boat ever to do so.

In 1883 the *Queen Victoria* was bought by Captain St. Amour and run between Chatham, Windsor and Detroit. At 4:00 a.m., September 13, 1883, six miles below Chatham, it was discovered to be on fire. It had been loading fuel. Members of the crew believed the fire was caused by a spark from the passsing barge, *Manitoba*.

Queen Victoria *on the Ottawa River, c. 1870. Public Archives of Canada, C 3721.*

The *Peerless*, which was licensed to carry 1,100 passengers, was the largest sidewheeler ever to sail the Ottawa River. It was originally built in England, taken apart, shipped to Canada in sections and reassembled in Ottawa in 1873. It had a completely iron hull, 202 feet long, 29 feet wide, and eight feet deep.

In 1886 the *Peerless* was rebuilt in Montréal and renamed the *Empress*. Shortened to 185 feet, it continued to run between Ottawa and Montréal as a regular mail steamer until it was scrapped in 1935.

This poster was used in the 1880s to acquaint the public with the four steamboats owned by the Ottawa River Navigation Company: the Peerless, *the* Princess, *the* Queen Victoria *and the* Prince of Wales. *Passengers could leave Ottawa at 7:30 a.m. or 5:00 p.m. on the* Peerless *or* Queen Victoria *for Montréal. The trip back upstream was made by train from Montréal to Lachine where passengers boarded the* Prince of Wales *or the* Princess *for the remainder of the journey. Public Archives of Canada, C 2259.*

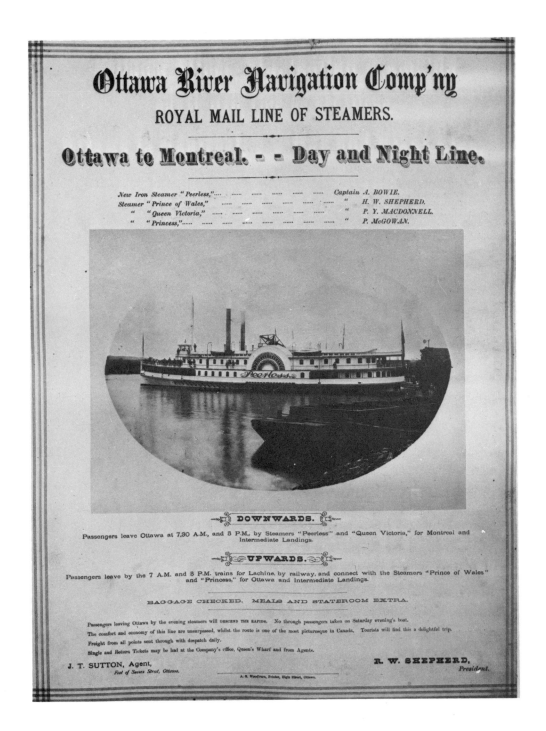

The *Atlas* was built in Carillon in 1869. It was 142 feet long, 22 feet wide and eight feet deep. It ran on the Ottawa River between Carillon and Montréal for the Ottawa River Navigation Company and for most of its life, it was a night passenger and freight boat. In 1874 it was rebuilt and named the *Princess,* travelling very often between Montréal and Point Fortune, Québec. The *Princess* was eventually laid up in 1913.

Public Archives of Canada, C 53671.

Empress, *formerly* Peerless, *in the Lachine Rapids. Notman Collection, McCord Museum.*

In 1866, the steamer *Dagmar* was built of
wood, probably at Carillon, for the Ottawa
River Navigation Company. It was 126 feet
long, 22 feet wide, with a six-foot draught.
The *Dagmar* carried passengers to ports along
the Ottawa River and to Montréal until
March 19, 1890, when it was destroyed by fire
at the wharf at Como, Québec. This picture
was taken circa 1875.

Public Archives of Canada, C 3719.

The *Maude* was built by Charles H. Gildersleeve at Kingston, Ontario, and launched
on August 16, 1871. It was christened by
Mr. Gildersleeve's young daughter. He sold it
in 1872 for excursion service around Kingston.
In 1894 the *Maude* was rebuilt at the Davis
Shipyard in Kingston, and lengthened to
153 feet and 33 feet wide. Its name was
changed to *America* and it was acquired by the
Canada Steamship Lines. In 1920 it was
bought by Newton K. Wagg of the Georgian
Bay Tourist Company and operated as a
propeller boat, the *Midland City*, until it was
broken up in 1955.

Maude *on the Ottawa River, c. 1900. Public
Archives of Canada, C3722.*

The *Filgate* was built in 1879 at Montréal. It was 158 feet long, had a 25-foot beam and an eight-foot depth, and weighed 263 tons. It carried passengers to ports along the St. Lawrence and Ottawa rivers until it burned at Valleyfield, Québec, on May 30, 1911. In our picture, the *Filgate*, heavily loaded with passengers, is driven by its walking beam engine through the Lachine Rapids in the late 1880s.

The *Sovereign* was built in 1889 in Montréal for the Ottawa River Navigation Company. It was 162 feet long, 26 feet wide, had a seven-foot draught, and weighed 635 tons. Its run was from Montréal to Carillon.

The Toronto *Daily Star*, March 19, 1906, reported that the *Sovereign*, which was known to thousands of Canadians, had burned to the water's edge at Lachine. It was a general favourite for moonlight festivities and short pleasure trips, frequently taking excursion parties up to the Lake of Two Mountains.

The fire was discovered at eleven o'clock in the men's sleeping quarters by a Mr. R. Roy who was awakened by the smell of smoke. Roy immediately aroused the others sleeping on board and someone telephoned the Lachine Fire Brigade. The fire on the boat, which was docked immediately in front of the local convent where 600 pupils were sleeping, set the sky aglow. The townspeople thought the convent was on fire.

The *Sovereign* was valued at $50,000, but only $40,000 in insurance was carried. It was rebuilt to 200 feet long, 42 feet wide and eight feet deep for a total weight of 1,098 tons. Renamed the *Imperial*, it was scrapped in 1928.

Filgate
Public Archives of Canada, C 4897.

Sovereign *on the Ottawa River, c. 1898.*
Ontario Archives.

The *G. B. Greene,* which was named after a former company president, was built for the Upper Ottawa Improvement Company in 1896 at Quyon, Québec. It was 142 feet long, 45 feet wide and eight feet deep. Twice as wide as a usual steamboat, it was originally designed to tow log booms on Lac Deschênes. Refitted to take excursion trips, the *G. B. Greene* came to be known as the "Queen of the River." It was damaged by fire in 1916.

The *Citizen* reported: *"The G. B. Greene is lost with four of the crew."*

"This well-known steamer burned at Quyon Dock causing the death of sleepers below decks. The pleasure steamer *G. B. Greene,* which is owned by the Upper Ottawa Improvement Company, and which has plied the waters of the Upper Ottawa River for over a quarter of a century, was burned to the water's edge at her berth at Quyon early yesterday morning. Four members of the crew, who were trapped below decks when the fire broke out, lost their lives.

"Owing to the age of the vessel, the fire spread so rapidly that no attempt could be made to stay its progress and the other members of the crew, ten in number, barely escaped with their lives by jumping overboard and swimming for shore.

"The fire was noticed about 1:20 a.m. by one of the deck hands, A. Gibson, who awoke to find the cabin full of smoke. He at once gave the alarm and, rushing to the deck, found the amidships part of the vessel a mass of flames which had burned the hawsers holding the vessel to the wharf.

"The boat was drifting out into the stream, with flames shooting from every part of her. So quickly did the fire spread through the ancient timbers that the crew, hurriedly awakened out of their slumbers, had to dash

through a barrier of flames and smoke to the deck.

"Captain John Chartier quickly saw that there was no hope of saving her and, putting his life belt around himself and his 14-year-old son, jumped with him into the water. Mrs. Fleury, the cook, who could not swim, was saved through the heroic efforts of her husband who put a life belt around her and towed her ashore, which he had at last managed to reach in an exhausted state.

"The names of the men who lost their lives are not at this time known. It is surmised that they did not realize their danger and stayed below in the cabin to save some of their effects and then were unable to reach the deck as their escape was cut off by flames which swept through the vessel in a few minutes. The

G. B. Greene on the Ottawa River, c. 1915. Public Archives of Canada, C 19826.

bodies which were recovered yesterday were badly burned.

"The burning steamer presented a thrilling picture as it slowly drifted out into the river, afire from one end to the other, the flames shooting high into the air from her superstructure. The reflection of the sky quickly brought a large number of residents to see this mass of flames. The cause of the conflagration is unknown but it is thought to have started in or near the engine room. . ."

The *G. B. Greene* was rebuilt again in 1917, and was not scrapped until 1947.

The G.B. Greene *under way. Public Archives of Canada, C 26381.*

The wreck of the G.B. Greene. *Public Archives of Canada, C 8592.*

Wrecked smokestack, engine and paddlewheel of the G.B. Greene. *Public Archives of Canada, C 31821.*

The Great Lakes

The first steamboat to navigate Lake Ontario was the *Frontenac,* which was launched on September 7, 1816, from Finkle's Point near Kingston. Its regular route was from Prescott to York (Toronto) and back in a week. The earliest steam vessels on Lake Erie were the *Chippewa* and the *Emerald,* which sailed prior to 1845. In 1838 the *Gore* was the first regular passenger steamer on Georgian Bay. It ran between Sturgeon Bay and Sault Ste. Marie. On Lake Huron the first steamer, the *Bruce Mines,* carried copper ore from the mines to Montréal. And the first steamer on Lake Superior was the propeller boat, the *Independent,* which travelled the south shore in 1844.

There were many casualties on the Great Lakes when shipbuilding was in its infancy. During the year 1871, for example, one thousand and sixty-seven disasters were recorded on the Lakes. There are however equally many tales of courageous rescue. The industry learned quickly from its losses, and safety precautions began to be enforced. This was made possible when large companies were formed with standard regulations for their ships. In the early days each ship was independently owned and operated, and many were of more or less experimental design. This made it extremely difficult to enforce any kind of safety code.

Up to 1837 the Lake Ontario steamers were unable to proceed further east than Kingston because of the rapids at Prescott. However, in 1838 they began docking at Prescott so that their passengers could take a stage coach past the Long Sault Rapids, and then another boat to Montréal. There were also many natural impediments to through navigation from the St. Lawrence River to Port Arthur. In spite of these obstacles, boat transportation was favoured because travel by road was gruelling. The leather-springed coaches bounced over rocky corduroy roads which, when wet, were transformed into slippery ooze. The roads were pitted and rutted by heavy ox-drawn freight wagons.

From Prescott to Montréal the St. Lawrence River was a series of non-navigable rapids. They were named "The Galops", "Coteau", "Cedars", "Split Rock", "Cascade" and "Lachine". It was not until lock systems bypassed these rapids that large boats could travel from Toronto to Montréal.

Two other natural barriers impeded navigation. The greatest of these was Niagara Falls, where the waters of Lake Erie poured into Lake Ontario. Freight on Lake Ontario landed at Queenston and was portaged across the Niagara Peninsula by heavy wagons to Chippewa on Lake Erie. There it was loaded onto boats and could proceed as far as Sault Ste. Marie, where it again had to be portaged to bypass rapids. These rapids were the second major obstacle to early shipping. Finally it was re-loaded onto boats to its destination at Port Arthur.

To eliminate the portage at Niagara, the Welland Canal was built. There were four Welland Canals in succession; each one deeper and wider than its predecessor. The first canal followed natural watercourses and was completed in 1829, the last was finished in 1929. The Sault Ste. Marie Canal was completed in 1855 and allowed steamers to sail from Lake Huron into Lake Superior.

The city of Toronto soon became the most important port west of Montréal. Its deep and naturally protected harbour was convenient to the Lake system, and the city's burgeoning industry made it a prime distribution point for manufactured and raw materials. Toronto was also the closest good Canadian port to the Erie Canal, which extended from Buffalo on Lake Ontario to New York City on the Atlantic Coast. The canal connected Rochester, Syracuse, Albany and the cities of the Hudson River. Using this route, merchants were able to send and receive goods efficiently between Ontario and New York.

Toronto eventually became the centre of commerce and shipbuilding, and the home port for all large Canadian boats on Lake Ontario. These boats generally travelled in a circular route along the north (Canadian) and south (American) shores of the Lake. They loaded and unloaded freight and passengers at Hamilton, Niagara, Buffalo, Rochester, Oswego, Ogdensburg, Prescott, Kingston, Picton, and finally back home at Toronto.

The sidewheeler *Frontenac* weighed 700 gross tons and was 170 feet long. It was built in 1816 by Teabout and Chapman at Ernestown on the Bay of Quinte at a cost of $20,000. The *Frontenac* was the first steamship to enter the Harbour of York (Toronto). Captained by James McKenzie, it ran regularly between Toronto and Prescott. It was damaged at Niagara in 1827 and broken up a few months later.

The Frontenac, *1817. Ontario Archives.*

Kingston, Toronto, Hamilton and Niagara
THE ROYAL MAIL STEAMERS

WILL LEAVE KINGSTON for COBOURG, PORT-HOPE and TORONTO, DAILY, (Sundays excepted) at 6 o'clock, P. M., on the arrival of the Mail Steamer from Montreal. The Steamer ECLIPSE leaves Toronto daily, (Sundays excepted) for Hamilton, at Half-past Two o'clock, P. M.

Fare from Kingston to Hamilton,—Cabin, $4½
do   do   do   Deck, $2
" from Kingston to Niagara, Cabin, $4½
"   do   do   Deck, $2
"   do   Toronto,   Cabin, $4
"   do   do   Deck, $2
" Kingston to Cobourg & Port-Hope, Cabin $2
"   do   do   do   Deck, $1

Returning, will leave Toronto Daily (Sundays excepted) on the arrival of the Mail Steamer Eclipse from Hamilton, at 12 o'clock, noon.

JOHN H. GREER, *Agent.*

Royal Mail Packet Office, Greer's Wharf,
Kingston, April 16, 1846.   30

Advertisement appearing in KINGSTON ARGUS *June 19, 1846.*

The *Passport* was built in 1846 on the Clyde River in Scotland. It had an iron hull 172 feet long, 25 feet wide and ten feet deep and weighed 346 tons. The steamer was then taken apart and transported to Kingston where it was reassembled and named the *Passport*. On June 1, 1847, it made its first run between Kingston and Montréal.

On June 27, 1847, at 9:00 p.m., en route from Montréal to Kingston, it grounded on a shoal, opposite Lancaster, Ontario. The engineer promptly shut off the engine, but he forgot to shut off the intake valve. This resulted in an accumulation of steam pressure which eventually blew live steam onto the deck among the passengers. Two people drowned. Forty-four others were seriously scalded; and 13 died from their burns.

In the early 1850s the *Passport* ran between Hamilton, Toronto and Montréal, and from 1845 on, it operated between Hamilton and Kingston, stopping at Port Hope and Cobourg.

On March 15, 1861, the *Passport* was sold to a Kingston company which almost immediately resold it to the Canadian Inland Steam Navigation Company. Around this time, the British Army was landing more troops in Canada. The 30th Cambridgeshire Regiment was transported from the Channel Islands to Québec City, where the regiment boarded the *Passport* for Toronto.

In 1875, the *Passport* was sold to the Richelieu and Ontario Navigation Company and continued on its route until 1898, at which time it was overhauled and modernized at Sorel. The original paddle wheel was replaced by feathering paddle wheels. Renamed the *Caspian*, the old vessel ran along the north shores of Lake Ontario during the years 1899 and 1900.

In 1901, the *Caspian* was sold to the Gildersleeve interests as a mate for their other ship,

The Passport *steaming through the Lachine Rapids, c. 1870. Public Archives of Canada, PA 28819.*

The Caspian, *Montréal Harbour, formerly the* Passport, *c. 1900. Public Archives of Canada, C 45425.*

the *North King*. In 1910, the *Caspian* operated between Deseronto, Kingston and across Lake Champlain to Charlotte, New York, which was at that time the lake port for Rochester.

In February, 1915, the Canada Steamship Lines came to own the *Caspian*. The *Caspian* continued in service for another six years and, in 1921, it was taken to the Canada Steamship Lines yards at Sorel and rebuilt as a tow barge.

The beautiful old sidewheeler, the *Europa*, was built in 1854 by the Harrison Company in Hamilton, Ontario, on the order of the W. P. Brown Company. The hull, which was made of wood, was 224 feet long, 28 feet wide and 13 feet deep. It was equipped with a vertical beam engine which drove paddle wheels 30 feet in diameter.

The *Europa* was designed to be a passenger, fast freight, and mail vessel on Lake Ontario. It ran between Hamilton, the Welland Canal and Niagara, making connections with the Great Western Railway until June, 1855, when it switched to the Hamilton, Ogdensburg, New York run.

On June 25, 1855, the *Europa* grounded on a shoal by Snake Island in the easterly end of Lake Ontario in a thick fog. Fortunately, there was no damage. In 1857 it was sold to a Montréal banker, Thomas Pattun, and its route changed to Toronto, Kingston, and Charlotte, Sacketts Harbour and Ogdensburg, New York.

In 1866, it was wrecked near Oswego. It is possible that the hull was rebuilt and that the *Europa* was eventually bought by the Richelieu and Ontario Navigation Company, which scrapped it in March of 1873.

The Europa *in Montréal Harbour, c. 1870. Public Archives of Canada, PA 43035.*

The Corinthian was built in Glasgow, Scotland, in 1864. It was 175 feet long, 27 feet wide and nine feet deep, weighing 374 tons, with a hull constructed of steel and iron. Its vertical beam engine drove paddle wheels 30 feet in diameter. It could make 17 miles an hour with 40 pounds pressure.

The Corinthian was originally built for Charles F. Gildersleeve of Kingston, Ontario, who operated it between Port Hope, Colborne, Cobourg and Rochester, New York. In 1868, it was sold to the Royal Mail Line. In 1869, it was again sold to the Canadian Inland Steam Navigation Company, which shifted its route to Montréal.

On July 7, 1874, the Corinthian was shooting the Cascade Rapids in the St. Lawrence River when it hit Split Rock. The 250 passengers were quickly transferred to the life boats and taken to shore. However, the hull was not damaged and the Corinthian was taken to Kingston where it underwent minor repairs.

In 1877, the new owners, the Richelieu and Ontario Navigation Company, rebuilt the steamer, increasing its tonnage to 614. For 15 years it made the Hamilton, Toronto, Kingston run without any problems. Then on September 20, 1892, while passing through the Côteau Rapids in the St. Lawrence River, it caught fire.

The Montréal Gazette, September 21, 1892 reported: "The great sensation of the street last night was the story from Coteau du Lac that the Richelieu and Ontario Navigation Company steamer Corinthian had been burned to the water's edge within a few miles of Lachine."

"The Corinthian had just passed the Cedar Rapids about half-past four when the second mate ran up from below and informed Captain Craig that the vessel was on fire.

"The Captain, who was on the bridge, ran down between decks and remained there some ten minutes. He discovered that part of the vessel in the vicinity of the smokestack was in flames. The hose was put to work and every effort made to subdue the fire. After seeing to these arrangements, the Captain again ascended to the promenade deck and requested that all passengers go aft.

"It was just then that the passengers discovered their peril. The flames had broken through the woodwork around the smokestack and were, just beyond, a raging conflagration. At this time the boat was about a mile from the shore and the Captain at once directed the pilot to beach her with as little delay as possible. All this time the Captain and crew exhibited admirable coolness. Owing to the many shoals, it was impossible to beach the boat immediately. The pilot, therefore, ran downstream for about half a mile, finally running the boat close into the shore within twenty feet of the bank.

"During this time, the life boats had been lowered in order to prepare for the last emergency. Happily, there was no necessity for the passengers to take to the boats, as the

Corinthian was run on the shore before the fire had gained headway. One of the boats was swung out between the ship and the shore and used as a bridge over which the passengers and the crew scrambled to safety.

"The *Corinthian* is now but a charred hull. Two minutes after the passengers were departed, she was a seething mass of flames, and even from the moment that the fire had been discovered, it was understood that nothing could save her. The sailors stuck to their posts until the vessel was safely beached, although surrounded by fire and smoke, and even then did not abandon their duty until they had emptied the boilers of water in order to prevent an explosion.

"Aboard the *Corinthian* when she left Kingston were seventy-five passengers of whom about half were women and children. There was also considerable freight being shipped from Toronto to Montréal, a great portion of this being fruit. All of this, with the Toronto passengers' baggage, had been destroyed and the only baggage saved was that taken off at Kingston. It was impossible to do anything more owing to the extreme rapidity with which the flames had spread.

"Mr. Charles F. Mansell of Toronto was one of the passengers on board the *Corinthian*. 'I was on the bow of the boat when I first noticed that something was wrong. And what I saw was a big tongue of flame leaping through the woodwork alongside the smokestack. At first, I thought it was from the smokestack itself but, just then, I saw the Captain get the message from the mate and knew there was something wrong. There was no excitement at all, for the Captain's coolness seemed to inspire all to confidence. The fire was discovered about half past four, we were beached at five, and ten minutes later the boat was on fire from stem to stern. I did not wait to see anything further, but got to Saint Dominic as fast as possible and from there into the city. If we had been out on the lake instead of close to shore when the fire broke out, I would not have had much confidence in our safety."

The *Norseman* was built in 1868 by the Cantin Company of Montréal for Charles Gildersleeve, a large shipowner and builder in Kingston. The hull was originally 154 feet long, 26 feet wide and ten feet deep. It travelled the Montréal, Toronto route until 1891 when it was rebuilt at Kingston to 175 feet long, and 43 feet wide. It was renamed the *North King*.

In 1917, the *North King* was bought by the Ontario Navigation Company which apparently restored its original name, *Norseman,* and put it on the Kingston, Toronto, Rochester and Port Hope route. It was scrapped in 1922.

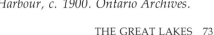

The North King, *also called the* Norseman, *in Kingston Harbour, c. 1900. Ontario Archives.*

The Norseman, *formerly the* North King.
Ontario Archives.

The *Argyle* was built in St. Catharines in 1872. It was a freight boat, 135 feet long, 23 feet wide, and had a 12-foot draught.

The Toronto *Globe,* June 15, 1906, reported that the *Argyle,* running between Lake Ontario ports, had been disabled on Saturday afternoon about a mile off Oshawa, by the breaking off of a portion of the walking beam. The passengers were transferred to the *Erindale,* maintained in a hotel in Oshawa over night, and returned by train to Toronto next day. The *Argyle* continued travelling regularly on this route until it became a barge in 1912.

The Argyle *at Port Colborne Harbour, c. 1875.*
Ontario Archives.

The *Frontier* was built at Mill Point, Ontario, in 1876 and launched under the name *Empress of India*. It was 170 feet long, 26 feet wide, with a nine-foot draught.

In 1899, the *Empress* was rebuilt at Picton, Ontario, lengthened to 185 feet, given a new hull number and renamed the *Argyle.*

In 1912, the hull was again rebuilt and named the *Frontier.* During 1913 it operated under the name *Grimsby,* but it was once again called the *Frontier* when it sank in the Detroit River in 1916.

The Empress of India, *also known as the* Argyle *and the* Frontier. *Public Archives of Canada, C 45398.*

The Frontier. *James Collection. City of Toronto Archives.*

The steel plates used to build the sidewheeler *Cibola* were precut in Glasgow, Scotland, then assembled at the Rathbun Boat Works at Deseronto, Ontario, in 1888. The hull was 252 feet long; the beam, 29 feet; and the draught, 12 feet. Its route included the American port of Lewiston, where it was eventually destroyed by fire, July 14, 1895.

Thunder Bay Historical Society Museum.

The *Corsican* was built in Montréal in 1870. It was 175 feet long and 27 feet wide. It was built as a passenger steamer to run between Montréal and Toronto. In 1905, its name was changed to *Picton*. It continued on this run until it burned in Toronto on September 21, 1907.

Corsican, *Montréal Harbour, c. 1871. Notman Collection, McCord Museum.*

The *Garden City* was built by the Bertram Shipyards in Toronto in 1892. Its hull was 178 feet long, its beam 26 feet and its draught 11 feet. It weighed 637 tons.

The *Garden City* operated on the Toronto to Dalhousie run for years without incident for the Niagara, St. Catharines and Toronto Navigation Company. It was finally scrapped in 1935.

The Garden City, *Port Hope Harbour, June 15, 1898. Ontario Archives.*

There were four boats on the Great Lakes named *City of Toronto.* The first was built in Niagara in 1839 and rebuilt in Detroit in 1863 and called the *Racine.* The *Racine* was rebuilt in Niagara in 1864 and at that time was named the *Algoma,* the second passenger ship of that name, and given a hull number. It was laid up in 1875 and scrapped in Collingwood in 1887.

The second *City of Toronto* was apparently also built in Niagara but in 1864. The third *City of Toronto,* the one in our picture, was built in Owen Sound in 1895. It travelled for most of its life on the Upper Great Lakes, calling at Niagara, Toronto, Penetang, Midland and Owen Sound. A fourth *City of Toronto* was built at Lauzon, Québec, in 1925, and laid up in 1959.

The City of Toronto *on Georgian Bay, c. 1927. K. E. Thro Collection.*

The *Alexandria* was built in Montréal in 1883. Its hull was 174 feet long, 31 feet wide and eight feet deep and its gross tonnage was 863. It was owned by the Richelieu and Ontario Navigation Company.

On Wednesday, August 4, 1915, the Toronto *Daily Star* reported the wreck of the *Alexandria*, which had taken place the preceding day. The wreck occurred during the worst storm on Lake Ontario in four years: the *Dalhousie City* had arrived in Toronto Harbour safely, but was three hours late; the *Chippewa* returned to port with a big hole in her hull caused by the violent waves; the *Carmona*, with 340 passengers, arrived in Toronto one hour late. The *Garden City* returned without completing its run, with many windows smashed and a large hole in the side of its hull. The *Corona* arrived from Niagara late and the *Modjeska* arrived from Hamilton late. The wind reached 40 miles per hour and the rainfall, calculated at 1:00 p.m. on August 3, was 485,624 tons.

The *Alexandria*, travelling from Montréal to Toronto under the direction of Captain W. M. Bloomfield, was loaded with its usual tonnage of coal for fuel. It began the run from Kingston under fine weather; nevertheless, at Port Hope, a storm arose such as neither the Captain nor the passengers had ever witnessed before. Despite all their power, the engines had to go flat out from Port Hope on, in order to keep the ship facing into the waves so that the Captain could steer it properly.

Steamer Alexandria *being painted, Niagara in background (1900-10). Ontario Archives.*

Alexandria. *Public Archives of Canada,* C 45401.

Because of the instability of the ship, and the amount of coal it was burning, the Captain ordered part of the cargo of sugar, pickles, potatoes, tomatoes, canned goods and used furniture thrown overboard to lighten the vessel. However, in the area of Scarborough Bluffs, the *Alexandria* ran out of coal and thus, lost power.

The only course left open to Captain Bloomfield was to attempt to beach his vessel on the sandy beach off the Bluffs. He ordered distress rockets fired and the life boats prepared as the *Alexandria* headed onto the shore. It grounded about two hundred feet off Scarborough Bluffs, just south of the present Stop Number 36 on Kingston Road and opposite what was then the property of the Deputy Reeve, J. E. O'Connell. O'Connell saw the rockets, heard the whistle, and took part in the rescue of the seamen. There were no passengers on this run.

By midnight, the people on the shore had a rescue line out to the freighter but the mighty steamer had already started to break up. By 5:00 a.m., 50 feet of the bow had broken away. The last person to abandon ship was Captain Bloomfield and the newspaper article tells of the heroism of the seamen and their rescuers who were, for the most part, farmers living above Scarborough Bluffs.

Wreck of the Alexandria, *1915, Toronto east end waterfront. James Collection, City of Toronto Archives.*

Wreck of the Alexandria. *Ontario Archives.*

Two vessels were registered in Canada under the name *Chippewa*. The steamer in our picture was built in 1893 at Hamilton, Ontario, according to a design by Frank E. Kirby of Detroit. It was 1,575 gross tons; 308 feet long; the beam, 36 feet; the draught, 14 feet. It was easily recognizable by its walking-beam engine between two tall stacks. The *Chippewa* provided spacious accommodation for over 2,000 passengers on the run between Toronto and Niagara for over 20 years. It was scrapped in Hamilton in 1939.

The sidewheeler *Corona* was built in Toronto in 1896. It was 270 feet long, had a 33-foot beam, a 13-foot draught, and weighed 1,274 tons. The ship's regular run was between Toronto and Niagara River ports, but it operated for several seasons between Toronto and Hamilton. It was withdrawn from service at the end of the 1929 season, and was scrapped in 1937.

The Corona, *in Toronto Harbour, c. 1920. James Collection, City of Toronto Archives.*

The Toronto, *Toronto Harbour, c. 1920. Public Archives of Canada, PA 33077.*

The sidewheeler *Toronto* was built in 1899 by the Bertram Shipyards in Toronto for the Richelieu and Ontario Navigation Company. It was 269 feet long, 36 feet wide, and 14 feet deep.

The *Toronto* maintained a summer service between Toronto, Rochester, N.Y., Kingston, Brockville, and Prescott. A sistership to the *Kingston*, both steamers had a beaver covered with gold leaf on the boxes of their paddle wheels. At Prescott, Montréal-bound passengers transferred to the rapids propeller steamers *Rapids King, Rapids Queen* or *Rapids Prince* to descend the rapids.

The ship was bought by Canada Steamship Lines in 1913 and continued its run until 1938. It was scrapped in 1947.

The Chippewa *with its unique pilot house and* two smokestacks. *Ontario Archives.*

Chippewa. *James Collection. City of Toronto Archives.*

A family scene aboard the Chippewa *while docked in Toronto Harbour, also showing its walking beam at rest. James Collection, City of Toronto Archives.*

Knapps Roller Boat, launched September 8, 1897, was probably the most unusual paddle wheel steamboat ever designed and built. Although the boat was unsuccessful in operation, its builder, F. A. Knapp, a flamboyant promoter, employed a most original concept. This boat was, in fact, one large cylindrical paddle wheel enclosing another cylinder which contained the passenger and motor compartments.

It was a tubular craft, 125 feet long and 25 feet in diameter on the outside. The two 60 horsepower engines were inside the inner cylinder, set on roller bearings at either end. They imparted a revolving motion to the tubular outer shell. Thus, both the engines and the passenger compartment in the centre remained relatively stationary.

Around the central part of the outer shell were horizontally-placed paddle-like projections. As the shell of the vessel revolved, these paddles would dig into the water and could propel the vessel around the Toronto harbour, at a purported speed of seven miles an hour. The vessel rolled sideways over the surface of the water.

On a glassy calm surface, it was said to operate at four or five miles per hour. However, it was very difficult to steer and, in fact, was unmanageable in rough water. Its passenger-carrying capacity was very limited. Around 1900, an unsuccessful attempt was made to turn it into a towing barge and it was abandoned at the foot of Sherbourne Street. Our photograph was taken in front of Polson's Ironworks where it had been built. It is now believed to lie buried under the Gardiner Expressway in Toronto.

The Polson Ironworks, established in 1883 by William Polson, had its shops at the foot of Sherbourne Street in Toronto on the lakeshore.

In 1888, Polson's opened a new shipbuilding yard in Owen Sound and began to construct the *Manitoba* which was to be a replacement vessel for the CPR steamer *Algoma* which had sunk on Lake Superior.

The Toronto plant flourished and soon extended on the waterfront from Sherbourne to Frederick Streets. By 1905, the staff numbered 450 and Polson's built numerous ocean-going ships for the Allies during the First World War. However, at the end of the war, shipbuilding declined in Canada and by 1919, Polson Ironworks filed for bankruptcy, having built over 150 large vessels for Cana-

Knapps Roller Boat *in the water being inspected. James Collection, City of Toronto Archives.*

dian and international companies. A new Toronto railway viaduct was constructed over the site of the Polson plant in 1920.

Although many of the rivers and lakes of the interior of Ontario have lower water levels today, they were once centres of commerce. The Thames River, which flows from London and empties into Lake St. Clair, was the most economical route for heavy freight for the settlers of south-western Ontario. The steamers of Lake Simcoe, Muskoka and the Kawarthas carried thousands of tons of freight, produce and timber, as well as early cottagers and adventurers. Sir John Franklin left from Penetanguishene Harbour for his last trip to the North Pole.

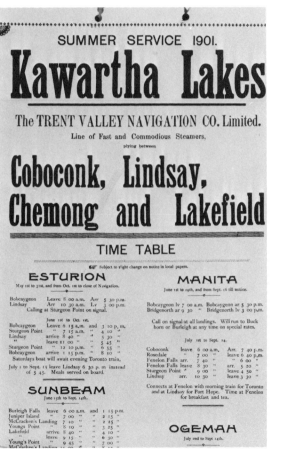

Top:
The City of Peterborough. *Public Archives of Canada, C 10302.*

Far Left:
The Trent Valley Navigation Co. Ltd. Kawartha Lakes Summer Service, 1901: Coboconk, Lindsay, Chemong and Lakefield. Public Archives of Canada, C7757.

Left:
Advertisement for the Georgina *which travelled between Penetang, Midland and Parry Sound. c. 1880. Huronia Museum, Midland, Ontario.*

The *Emily May* was the largest and most serviceable sidewheeler on Lake Simcoe. It was built of rare blue oak at Belle Ewart, Ontario, in 1861. Its hull was 144 feet long, with a 21-foot beam and an eight-foot draught. The *Emily May* could carry 800 passengers and travel at 14 miles per hour. It was owned by a Captain May, and named after his daughter Emily.

The steamer's route was from Belle Ewart to Orillia, making connections with the Northern Railway and debarking passengers and freight at different points on Lakes Simcoe and Couchiching. The *Emily May* was sold to the North Simcoe and Huron Railway and in 1874 renamed *Lady of the Lakes.* After 21 years of service, in 1882, it burned, and was scrapped.

The *Ida Burton* was built at Orillia, Ontario, and launched on June 15, 1866. The hull was 82 feet long, 14 feet wide, with a six-foot draught. The 45 horsepower engine, which was built by S. Whitney of North Orillia, drove the boat at 12 miles per hour.

The launching ceremony was attended by almost one thousand people. Shortly after the workmen began to remove the supports, a Miss Oliver broke the customary bottle of claret and wished success to the *Ida Burton.* After the steamer was moored to the wharf, workmen and friends were fêted with a barrel of ale.

The *Ida Burton* ran daily between Barrie, Orillia and the Severn River, connecting with the Northern Railway and the stagecoaches. It supplied the most direct and pleasant route between Toronto and the holiday region of Muskoka. The extension of the railway was the death blow to the regular steamboat passenger business, relegating the steamboats to towing and excursions. We last hear of the *Ida Burton* in 1875.

Sidewheeler Emily May *at dock in Orillia, Ontario, c. 1870. Simcoe County Archives.*

The sidewheeler Ida Burton *at dock, Orillia, Ontario. Simcoe County Archives.*

The *Wenonah* was built by A. P. Cockburn in 1866 at Gravenhurst, Ontario. It was 81 feet long, 16 feet wide with a six-foot draught. It travelled at ten miles per hour on the Muskoka Lakes between Gravenhurst and Bracebridge.

In 1877, the *Wenonah* was refitted and lengthened to 99 feet. In 1885 it was retired, and the engines were removed and installed in a new steamer on the Magnetawan River. The hull was left to decay on Cinderwood Island.

The wooden-hulled sidewheeler *Nipissing* was built at Gravenhurst, Ontario, in 1871, with a vertical beam engine, which would drive it 14 miles per hour. It was 110 feet long, 18 feet wide, with a seven-foot draught. It was originally designed as a copy of a larger steamer, the *Emily May*.

In 1872, the *Nipissing* sailed only on Lake Muskoka, but it was able to travel to Gravenhurst, Port Carling, Lake Rosseau and Port Cockburn. In 1877 it was rebuilt at Gravenhurst. A hurricane deck was added and the passenger capacity was enlarged from 148 to 243.

Early in the morning of August 3, 1866, fire was discovered on the *Nipissing*. To protect other vessels in Port Cockburn, the blazing hull was cut free. It drifted off into the lake, running aground on a nearby island. The hull burned to the water line and finally sank.

The boiler and engines were salvaged and transferred to a new steamer, the *Nipissing II*, which was very similar in appearance to the original *Nipissing*, but which had a hull made of iron on the River Clyde in Scotland. The hull was shipped in sections to Gravenhurst to be reassembled. This original iron hull can still be seen today. It was eventually made into the propeller ship *Segwun* which is now being rebuilt in Gravenhurst.

Wenonah, *Gravenhurst, Ontario. Ontario Archives.*

Nipissing II, *rebuilt in 1877. Ontario Archives.*

The wreck of the *Victoria* on the Thames River near London, Ontario, is one of our worst maritime disasters. The *Victoria* was one of three ships running between London and Springbank, a charming park five miles from London. It was a flat-bottomed sternwheeler, some 60 feet long, with upper and lower decks. The lower deck was surrounded by a canopy.

On May 24, 1881, as it returned overladen with passengers from Springbank Park, the engine broke loose and slid off the lower deck, carrying away with it the supports for the upper deck. The upper deck and the canopy then fell down upon the people crowded on the lower deck, and held them, so that they were unable to escape. Over 182 people were drowned or crushed. The *Victoria* suddenly lifted to one side and sank in ten feet of water, near Coverbridge.

Building the steamer Victoria *on the banks of the Thames River, London, Ontario. Ontario Archives.*

The sunken wreck of the Victoria, *Thames River, London, Ontario, 1881. Ontario Archives.*

Right Hand Page:
The Chicora *taking on fuel at Killarney in Georgian Bay, c. 1870. Public Archives of Canada, C 3947.*

Two passenger ships, each bearing the name *Algoma*, traded from Lake Huron and Georgian Bay to Lake Superior over a century ago.

The sidewheeler *Algoma*, in our photograph, was originally named the *City of Toronto* and was built in 1839 at Niagara-on-the-Lake for the Royal Mail Line to operate on Lake Ontario. It had a wooden hull 147 feet long, 23 feet wide, with a 12-foot draught. It weighed 500 tons.

The two engines, made by Ward's Eagle Foundry, Montréal, were vertical beam engines with cylinders 46 inches in diameter, a 12-foot stroke and two return flue boilers. The paddle wheels were 26 feet in diameter.

The *City of Toronto* was one of the very first steamers on the Great Lakes to have double vertical beam engines, an engineering feature that enabled it to turn easily. Also, it was originally built with a clipper bow, a square stern and three tall masts for sails.

When the *City of Toronto* was first launched, it had no upper cabins, all passenger accommodation being between decks. Its first years were spent in passenger service between Kingston and Prescott. Then, in 1843, it was transferred to the Toronto, Niagara, Queenston, Buffalo and Lewiston, New York route. In April 1842, Charles Dickens was a passenger, going as far as Kingston, where he took another steamer to Toronto.

At that time, the fare from Lewiston to Kingston was $5 including berth and meals. A passenger could make the trip for $2 if he was content to sleep on the deck and bring his own food.

In 1863, the *City of Toronto* was damaged by fire while in Niagara and the hulk was consequently sold to Ward of Detroit, Michigan. In order to get the vessel through the Welland Canal, much of it had to be disassembled. It was then towed to Detroit where it was

completely rebuilt. The ship was much changed in appearance but it retained the original engines. Named the *Racine*, it was registered as an American vessel and operated between Detroit and Lake Michigan ports.

In 1865 it returned to Canada and was renamed the *Algoma*. The following years were prosperous ones. The steamer had no serious accidents and it made money for the owners. It was the pioneer steamer of the Collingwood, Lake Superior area, and of the Royal Mail Line, owned at that time by Toronto interests. It commenced weekly trips to Bruce Mines and Sault Ste. Marie, calling at Georgian Bay ports. A second route was to Thunder Bay (Prince Arthur's Landing), with calls at Hudson's Bay Company posts on Lake Superior.

The *Algoma* was used as a troop ship and on May 27, 1870, landed the first contingent going

The Algoma *at Port Arthur docks. Note its double walking beam engines, c. 1875. Public Archives of Canada, C 28537.*

to quell the Métis Uprising in Red River. The *Algoma* continued to sail into Prince Arthur's Landing regularly until the fall of 1871. It was then tied up in Collingwood Harbour and kept idle until August, 1874, when it, for one day only, acted as an escort to the *Chicora* which had been chartered by Governor-General Lord and Lady Dufferin who were visiting the Upper Great Lakes.

The *Algoma* again lay idle and rotting at the dock until a day in 1881 when it caught fire. The burning hulk drifted across the harbour and embedded itself near the old dock of a lumber firm.

The *Ploughboy* was built by Captain W. Eberts at the Eberts Shipyards in 1851 at Chatham, Ontario. Its hull was made of wood, 170 feet long by 28 feet wide by eight feet deep. It weighed 450 gross tons. The engine of the *Ploughboy*, which had been made by the Ward Ironworks in Montréal, had been originally installed in the *Transit* which was dismantled in 1850. It was a side lever engine with a cylinder 42 inches in diameter and a stroke of four feet six inches. The paddle wheels were 24 feet in diameter.

From 1851 to 1864 the *Ploughboy* was owned by the Park Brothers of Amherstburg, Ontario. On October 1, 1851, they began making daily excursions between Chatham, Amherstburg and Detroit. In April 1854, the Great Western Railroad was completed from Niagara to Windsor, passing through Chatham, providing a direct rail service from the east to Chicago. The *Ploughboy* was no longer necessary for transportation in this area.

The *Ploughboy*, in 1856, under the command of Captain Rowan, was the first steamer to take regular passenger and freight service to Lake Huron ports beyond Goderich. There were no navigation lights north of Goderich and very few places had adequate docks. Sailing a ship in these waters was a precarious undertaking.

When the *Ploughboy* stopped at Kincardine a large scow had to be rowed out to take off passengers and freight. If the water was rough, the passengers and freight were unable to land. So, in 1856, the Department of Public Works began the construction of two piers which were to give adequate docking facilities for several years.

By 1859 the *Ploughboy*'s route had been extended to Owen Sound and Collingwood. The *Kaloolah* and the *Ploughboy* in the 1850s were the first large freight and passenger

ships to serve the Georgian Bay area. From this time on, the *Ploughboy* travelled over the Great Lakes, calling at ports such as Buffalo, Port Stanley, Detroit, Windsor, Sarnia, Goderich, Owen Sound, Meaford, Collingwood and Penetanguishene.

On the morning of July 2, 1859, with Sir John A. Macdonald on board, the *Ploughboy* left Collingwood for Sault Ste. Marie. As it was approaching Lonely Island in Georgian Bay, an engine breakdown occurred. The ship's officers were immediately aware of the peril. Without power, the battered *Ploughboy* was being driven closer and closer to the treacherous rocks off Lonely Island.

The anchor was dropped. It dragged along the bottom of the lake for over twelve miles. The passengers gave up all hope and prepared to meet what appeared to be inevitable disaster. It was felt that a religious service should be held, as many of the passengers believed they would die, but none felt equal to the task of conducting the service. Finally a government

Ploughboy, July 2, 1859, 50 yards from the rocks of Lonely Island. Metropolitan Toronto Library Board.

official read a petition from an Anglican Prayer Book for those in peril on the sea.

By 2:30 the next morning, the *Ploughboy* was within 50 yards of the rocky shore. Suddenly, the anchors bit into the rugged floor of the bay and held. The ship remained firm until the following midnight when the lights of an approaching vessel were seen. Help had arrived. Five crew members had rowed a life boat 70 miles to Owen Sound. The steamer *Canadian* was contacted and, as quickly as possible, it rushed to the aid of the *Ploughboy*. The crippled *Ploughboy* was taken in tow and all persons were landed safely at Collingwood.

Sir John A. Macdonald later wrote, "You will see by the papers what a narrow escape we had. None of the party will be nearer to their graves until they are placed in them. The people behaved well, the women heroically."

In August, 1863, one of the passengers on the *Ploughboy* was found murdered in his cabin. This crime was never solved. In 1864, the *Ploughboy* was sold, renamed the *T. F. Park*, and converted into a tug on the Detroit River. In 1870 it became a freighter, operating between Port Stanley and Cleveland, Ohio. On June 3, 1870, the hull, again called the *Ploughboy*, burned while moored in Detroit Harbour. It was a total loss and inadequately covered by insurance.

The *Kaloolah*, an all-wooden sidewheeler, was built at Buffalo, New York, in 1853. It was 188 feet long, 25 feet wide, 10 feet deep, with 26-foot paddle wheels. It was named after the heroine of what had been a contemporary best-selling novel. It first operated between Buffalo, Port Stanley and ports on Lake Erie.

Later in 1853 the *Kaloolah* was sold to Charles Thompson of Collingwood. Renamed the *Collingwood*, its route was from Sault Ste. Marie to Midland. It was the first Canadian paddlewheeler to venture onto Lake Superior.

In 1858, the *Collingwood* was rebuilt in Detroit and given its original name, the *Kaloolah*. It was chartered to transport the Hinde Geological Expedition to explore the Canadian west. After passing through Sault Ste. Marie on July 27, 1858, it encountered a storm on Lake Superior which blew it up on Michipicoten Island. A member of the Expedition made this drawing.

The *Kaloolah* was reconditioned during that winter. It continued its old route until 1860 when it began running to Port Elgin, Saugeen, Michigan, and Kincardine, Ontario.

The *Kaloolah* came to a noble end. During a storm on August 22, 1862, while attempting to save sailors from the foundering *Charles Napier*, the *Kaloolah* was driven onto the beach and broken in half.

Ploughboy *taken 1856 by Collingwood's first elevator. Thunder Bay Historical Museum Society.*

The Collingwood, *formerly the* Kaloolah, *aground on Michipicoten Island, July 28, 1857. Metropolitan Toronto Library Board.*

The *Philo Parsons* was built of wood by Charles Heineman of Algonac, Michigan, in 1861. It was 135 feet long, 20 feet wide and had paddle wheels 27 feet in diameter. It was powered by a vertical beam engine with a 40-inch diameter cylinder and a nine-foot stroke.

During the American Civil War, two groups of Confederate soldiers were ordered to attack the Northern States by way of Canada.

The *Philo Parsons* ran regularly between ports on the American and Canadian sides of the Detroit River. On September 19, 1864, it left Detroit on its way to Sandusky, Ohio. At the ports of Sandwich and Malden, Ontario, a total of 34 more passengers came on board. They were all young, alert, quiet, self-composed young men who kept to themselves during the trip. They were actually soldiers in the Confederate Army. They had secretly come into Canada, and assembled in the Windsor area.

Nearing Kelly Island, the men positioned themselves at strategic places on the ship. At a given signal they drew their revolvers and seized control of the *Philo Parsons*. They made a stop to refuel at Middle Bass Island where they captured another vessel, the *Island Queen*, which innocently happened alongside.

The Confederate soldiers next planned to capture the American gunboat *Michigan*, which they would use to attack the prison at Johnson's Island near Sandusky, Ohio. This prison held a large number of captured Confederate soldiers who would be liberated and brought to freedom in Canada. The passengers and crew of the *Island Queen* were taken aboard the *Philo Parsons* and the *Island Queen* was scuttled in Lake Erie.

In the meantime, another group of Confederates were preparing to attack the gunboat *Michigan* by land, an attack which would

The *Philo Parsons. K.E. Thro Collection.*

coincide with the *Philo Parsons'* attack by sea. All of these men, if captured in civilian clothes, would have been shot as spies.

The *Philo Parsons* awaited for the signal which would tell of a successful attack on the gunboat but it never came. Instead, the Confederates on the *Philo Parsons* saw much activity which indicated to them that their plan had failed. The *Philo Parsons,* now under the control of the Confederate Army, fled to the Canadian shore.

At Malden, Ontario, some of the Confederate soldiers fled into Canada. The rest abandoned the *Philo Parsons,* rowed into the harbour at Sandwich, Ontario, and disappeared. The crew and passengers of the late *Island Queen* were left stranded on Fighting Island. The *Philo Parsons* was eventually towed back to the United States.

The ship was eventually berthed at a pier in Chicago where it was destroyed by the Great Chicago fire of 1871. It holds the distinction of being the only Confederate naval vessel to operate in Canadian waters against the Northern States.

The Chicora; *note its unique pilot house and the characteristic position of the smokestacks, c. 1870. Toronto Harbour Commission Archives.*

The *Chicora* was built by William C. Miller and Company of Birkenhead, England, in 1864. The engines were built by Laird Bros., also of Birkenhead. The hull was made of steel, 221 feet long, 26 feet wide and with a ten-foot draught. It weighed 930 tons. The side lever engine had cylinders which were 52 inches in diameter and with a four-foot stroke. They were rated at 180 horsepower. The paddle wheels were 28 feet in diameter.

The original name of this vessel was the *Letter B*. It was built to be a blockade runner in the American Civil War for the Confederacy and was similar in all respects to a previous blockade runner, the *Letter A*. It was commissioned by Mr. Henry Lafone of Nassau, British West Indies, and the Chicora Import and Export Company of Charleston, South

Carolina, which were agents for the Confederate Government. It was launched in February, 1864, and arrived in Bermuda, having changed its name to *Chicora*, on April 22, 1864.

The *Chicora* made a number of successful runs through the blockade to the Southern States during the next three months. On February 17, 1865, the Confederates evacuated Charleston. The *Chicora* happened to be in port. It made good its escape and sailed to Nassau. It later fled to Halifax, chased by several Northern gunboats.

Interned in Halifax until the end of the War, the *Chicora* was purchased February 27, 1866, by Benjamin Wier. The new owner sent it up the St. Lawrence River to Montréal, where it was cut in half and laid up at Sorel during the winter of 1867–8. The *Chicora* was transported

in two sections to Kingston, arriving May 2, 1868, a ten-day segment of a much longer voyage. In August, 1868, at Bells Shipyard in Buffalo, the two sections were rejoined. The *Chicora* was then sailed to Collingwood, Ontario, arriving September 7, 1868.

During that winter, lounges, cabins and staterooms were rebuilt and the ship was refinished as a passenger steamer. In the spring of 1869, the *Chicora* went on the Collingwood, Fort William, Lake Superior and Manitoulin run.

In 1870 it was used to transport troops and equipment for Colonel Garnet Wolseley, a British general, who led the fledgling Canadian army in its attack upon the Métis in Red River. The Wolseley Expedition also returned to Collingwood on the *Chicora*.

In 1873 the *Chicora* was laid up, remaining inactive until July, 1874, when it was chartered by the Government of Canada as a yacht for an inspection trip by Governor-General Lord Dufferin of the north shores of Lake Huron and Lake Superior. When they returned to Collingwood, the *Chicora* was once again laid up.

In April, 1877, the Niagara Navigation Company was formed and it purchased the *Chicora*. The vessel's upper works were taken off and shipped by rail to Toronto. The hull was towed on August 5, 1877, to Port Colborne, through the Welland Canal as far as the lock at Port Dalhousie.

There, a problem arose. How would they fit a 230-foot hull into a 200-foot lock? The two parts of the hull were rejoined and floated stern-first into the lock. The upper gates of the

Waubuno *in Collingwood Harbour. c. 1875.*
Thunder Bay Historical Museum Society.

lock were left open, adding 33 feet to the
length of the lock. Then the water was gradually drawn off from the lock itself, as well as
from a five-mile stretch of canal to St. Catharines. In ten days, the water level in the
lock and canal were the same height as Lake
Ontario and the *Chicora* was floated out. It was
then towed to Toronto where the Robb Shipyards installed the wheels and wheel guards.

On May 24, 1878, the *Chicora* made a round
trip from Toronto to Hamilton and, on June 1,
went on the regular Toronto, Queenston,
Lewiston run, being the very first boat purchased by the Niagara Navigation Company.
After 1884, the *Chicora* was the only boat on
the Niagara, Toronto run in regular service.
Then, in the spring of 1888, the company built
the *Cibola* at Deseronto, Ontario, and put it on
the same route.

In 1890, the *Chicora* was overhauled,
modernized, given new boilers, and the
engines were rebuilt. It continued, then, on
the Toronto, Queenston, Lewiston run.

In 1920 the hull of the *Chicora* was rebuilt as
a barge and named the *Warrenko*. It saw service
in and around Kingston Harbour until it sank
in a collision in June, 1939.

The *Waubuno* was a sidewheeler built of wood
at Port Robinson, Ontario, in 1865. Its engine,
a vertical beam, was built in Collingwood. The
hull was 135 feet long, 18 feet wide and seven
feet deep. It was owned by the Beatty family of
Thorold, Ontario, and used to transport supplies between Collingwood, Parry Sound, and
various ports on Georgian Bay and Lake
Huron. "*Waubuno*" means "soft west wind" in
Ojibway.

Collingwood was the transfer terminal for
supplies going to the Upper Great Lakes for
the Northern Railway which ran from Toronto.
The *Waubuno*'s sister ship on this route was the
Algoma and both steamers were owned by the
Great Northern Transit Company.

In 1867, the *Waubuno* carried the survey
party led by a famous Canadian surveyor,
James Dawson, on his way to survey the

Dawson Route from present day Thunder Bay
to Lake Winnipeg.

On November 21, 1879, the *Waubuno* was
loading supplies at Collingwood which were
consigned to Parry Sound when a northwest
gale and snowstorm came up. This postponed
the departure.

Among the passengers who spent the night
at the local hotel were a young doctor and his
bride. During the night, the bride had a dream
of a ship being wrecked and it so terrified her
that she persuaded her husband not to take
the boat.

The *Waubuno* left Collingwood at 4:00 a.m.
the next day, Saturday, November 22, 1879, as
the storm had died down. However, during
the day, another terrible storm arose and
nothing was seen of the *Waubuno* again.

It was not until March 30, 1880, that the capsized hull of the *Waubuno* was found by a search party in the shallow water behind Moose Point. Little was left, the main deck had been torn out and the machinery was gone. Twenty-four persons lost their lives but none of the bodies were ever recovered. There were no survivors and though the wreckage of the vessel remains to this day accessible to skin divers, there has never been any explanation as to what happened that stormy night.

The Sarnia *Canadian Observer* reported November 25, 1879:

"The loss of the steamer *Waubuno* is the most mysterious tragedy in the inland waters of Canada.

"During the 1870s the *Waubuno* ran between Collingwood and Parry Sound, making two round trips a week. It had three captains since going into service, Captain Symes, Captain Black Pete Peters, and finally Captain J. Burkett who perished with his vessel...

"Only one person in the entire world saw the *Waubuno* after her lights vanished in the darkness of Collingwood harbour. He was the lighthouse keeper on Christian Island who recognized the lights of the *Waubuno* as she passed in the gloom of the night. Some hours later, lumbermen working near the Moon River, heard a steamboat's whistle and recognized it as that of the *Waubuno*. From the direction of the sound, they concluded that the Captain was trying to get into the calmer waters of the South Channel by way of the reef known as the Haystack Rocks."

After the *Waubuno* failed to arrive at Parry Sound, a lumber company sent a tug, the *Bittie Grew*, to search the South Channel. The tug's crew found a life boat and some wreckage. All about, on the numerous small islands, were quantities of the freight that the *Waubuno* had been carrying. The Indians and whites were said to have fought over the plunder.

"The next year, when navigation opened, a party from Collingwood went to the scene of the wreck seeking, if possible, to recover some of the bodies, but they found none. Strangely, all the life preservers had been recovered, none having been used, an indication that the disaster had happened suddenly and apparently without warning."

The *Daily Globe*, Tuesday, November 25, 1879 reported, "Mr. A. Cadotte reports that while coming down the Georgian Bay yesterday, he passed portions of the cabin and decks of the steamer *Waubuno,* also barrels of flour coming from the western islands. He said that the north shore is strewn with portions of the wreck and the cargo."

On November 26, at 11:30 p.m. Mr. George MacLean of the Guelph Lumber Company arrived from Parry Sound into Toronto by way of Gravenhurst. He found, near Moose Point, a piece of board which bore the letters "WA" which he recognized as part of the *Waubuno*'s paddle box. A framed picture known to have hung in the Captain's cabin, a sofa and other articles also drifted in and had been thrown up onto the rocks. He stated that the shore in the centre was strewn with magnificent apples; their barrels were probably washed off the deck of the *Waubuno*.

Today travellers can explore the area where the *Waubuno* met her fate. It is south of Parry Sound, a few miles north of 12 Mile Bay. Waubuno Harbour is a shallow, rocky, treacherous bay guarded by the appropriately named Wreck Island.

The sidewheeler *Frances Smith* was launched at Owen Sound on April 30, 1867, being christened by Charlotte Cornelia Smith, the eleven-year-old grandchild of her owner-captain, who named the ship after his wife. It was built of wood by M. Simpson: 182 feet long, 28 feet wide and a 12-foot draught. Its engine had been originally installed in the *Gildersleeve* in Kingston in 1839, and the *Clifton* in 1854.

Initially the *Frances Smith* ran from Owen Sound to Collingwood. When the Toronto Grey and Bruce Railway provided Owen Sound with direct railway service to Toronto, the ship was placed on the route from Collingwood and Owen Sound to Port Arthur. At one time it was owned by the Beatty Company of Sarnia. In 1870 it was chartered with the *Algoma* to carry soldiers and supplies for Colonel Garnet Wolseley from Collingwood to Port Arthur to assist in the first battle against Louis Riel.

On October 29, 1875, the *Frances Smith* had a close call. It began to leak badly on Lake Superior and the crew had to drive the cargo of sheep and cattle overboard to save the ship.

In 1877 it was sold to the Lake Superior Transportation Company. When the railroads reached the North Shore of Lake Superior, the boat traffic dropped off and various companies amalgamated, becoming the Northern Navigation Company in 1888. At this time they repaired the *Frances Smith* and renamed it the *Baltic*.

September 5, 1889, the Owen Sound *Advertiser* reported: "*Ship of Terror, Five Persons Under Arrest*".

"The following tragic events occurred aboard the steamer *Baltic* on her last trip. A young man named Charles Hambly was accused of an unmentionable crime and with-

The Frances Smith *at the L. S. & M. Docks, Duluth, Minnesota, c. 1875, with the U.S. propeller boat, the* Meteor. *Thunder Bay Historical Museum.*

out waiting to investigate a number of the crew determined to tar and feather the lad.''

What was the crime?

Charles Hambly was, according to his father, Thomas Hambly of Albemarle Township, County of Bruce, ''A sober quiet boy of peaceable disposition.'' He was 17 years old, five feet five inches tall, unbearded, had curly brown hair, had never touched a drop of liquor in his life, and was proud of his membership in the Wiarton Sons of Temperance Lodge. He was used to hard work, having helped on the family farm since he was a child. After the last stook of hay was in the barn and all the crops were in, he walked to Wiarton, then rode to Owen Sound and hired on as a deck hand on the *Baltic*.

On September 19 the Owen Sound *Advertiser* reported the preliminary trial of Thomas Russell, second engineer, Aaron Tripp, first cook, George Dagget, second cook, and Kenneth McFadden, second porter.

''Passenger J. T. McInnis stated that he was on the deck of the *Baltic* when he noticed a number of people running forward. He joined them and arrived at the scene of the confusion where he saw 'A young man in tar and feathers stripped stark naked. They [the ship's crew] seemed to be having a little run with him. They led him around for a while and asked people if they had seen the show.' ''

Hector Lamont of Collingwood related, ''I spoke to one of the waiters in the cabin and he said to me, 'Have you seen what the boys have been doing downstairs?' I followed him to the

fore part of the ship and saw a man blackened with feathers sticking to him.''

''The boy seemed to be exhausted and he was caught up by the hair and chucked under the chin. I said it was a shame.'' Here Lamont broke down in his testimony and began to cry.

John Baxter was the next witness. He related that the boy sat alone after his torment, naked and confused. The Captain approached the lad and ordered him into his clothes, to pack his bag, draw his pay and leave the *Baltic* at the next port, which would have been Colpoy's Bay. ''He did not seem to be right, I thought him to be insane.'' The next sound Baxter heard was the splash of Hambly's body as he dashed overboard.

The crew of the *Baltic* were a rough, semi-literate, hard-drinking band of sailors. Hazing and harassment of new young sailors, was a common practice on Great Lakes ships of the time.

The Great Northern Transportation Company was later absorbed by Canada Steamship Lines. The *Baltic* burned while docked in Collingwood on September 5, 1895. Hughie Myler of Collingwood used wood from the ship's rudder to carve the model of the *Frances Smith* which is in the Collingwood Museum.

A stained glass window in St. Georges Anglican Church in memory of Captain Smith won a first prize during the Chicago World's Fair.

Cumberland, *Collingwood, c. 1875. Thunder Bay Historical Museum Society.*

The *Cumberland,* a sidewheeler, was built by Melancthon Simpson at Port Robinson, Ontario, for the Lake Superior Navigation Company in 1871. It was named after Fred Cumberland, manager of the Great Northern Railway at that time. It was 205 feet long, had a 26-foot beam with a draught of 11 feet. It contained a vertical beam engine with a piston 44 inches in diameter and a 132-inch stroke. This engine was originally built in 1847 by the R. H. Dunham Company, in New York, and installed in the *Cataract* and then the *Columbia.*

The *Cumberland* made its first voyage in October, 1871, and travelled that year between Collingwood and Fort William on Lake Superior. In November, 1872, it was frozen in the ice in Bear Lake. Captain Orr and four of his crew then left the steamer in charge of the first mate and walked over the ice along the

north shore of Georgian Bay for 20 days to Collingwood. The steward, stewardess and two waiters were left on board and endured great privation.

On November 7, 1874, while on western Lake Superior, the *Cumberland* lost caulking and began to leak. To save the ship, 75 head of cattle had to be driven overboard. The *Cumberland* was badly damaged and was lucky to reach Prince Arthur's Landing. It had only been at the dock for a few hours when suddenly it sank. It was raised, repaired and ran during the seasons 1876 and 1877.

The *Sentinel,* published at Price Arthur's Landing on July 26, 1877, reported: "The *Cumberland* toward the close of last week was due here, and not arriving Sunday or Monday, some uneasiness was felt. However, she arrived Tuesday morning, July 24, and reported she had been delayed on a bar in Nipigon Harbour for three days."

As it set out for Duluth, the *Cumberland* met an American boat also going there. As the

captain was worried about the seaworthiness of his ship, he transferred his passengers. The *Cumberland* started back towards Collingwood, struck Rock of Ages Reef near Isle Royale and stuck fast.

The steamer, high and dry, and laden with merchandise, was grounded with about four feet of water in its hold. The *Cumberland* must have been making good speed at the time as it was reported to have "run on so hard that all the forward half of the vessel is on the reef." If it had run just half its length to the left or right, it would have cleared without incident.

Apparently the shoal area where it was stranded was "not laid down on the Canadian charts" in use at the time. Rumours spread on both sides of the blue water boundary that Captain Parsons and the *Cumberland* were "led into the scrape by relying on the charts of Lake Superior furnished by the United States."

Office of the U.S. Lake Survey
Detroit, Michigan,
August 11, 1877

To the Editor of the Detroit *Daily Post*:

It has been stated that the steamer *Cumberland* grounded near Isle Royale at a point where the charts show 60 feet of water.

I send you herewith the United States Lake Survey Chart of Isle Royale, and a copy of a letter from the owners of the *Cumberland,* showing where the steamer was lost.

You will see that our chart distinctly indicates six (6) feet of water and rock bottom at the point where the vessel struck.

It seems that the Canadian chart is at fault, and not the chart of the United States Lake Survey.

Very Respectfully,
/S/ H. M. Adams,
Captain of Engineers.

"Although several tugs and steamers have been pulling at her, they did not succeed in getting her off. . . ." Salvage hopes remained high, though, since "wrecking tugs and apparatus were sent for, to Detroit, and should the lake continue quiet, it is possible that she may be saved."

The *Cumberland* was abandoned to the elements by the wreckers on August 6, amidst foul weather. The crew were taken aboard the *Frances Smith* and returned to Collingwood, where the *Cumberland* was declared a total loss of $50,000 plus cargo.

The well-known Great Lakes passenger steamer, the *Manitoba*, was built of wood in 1871 at Port Robinson, Ontario, by the Simpson Shipyards for J. H. W. Beatty of Sarnia. It was 173 feet long with a 25-foot beam and an 11-foot draught. It was driven by a vertical beam engine having a piston 45 inches in diameter with a 100-inch stroke.

The *Manitoba* ran from Sarnia to Lake Superior. On July 11, 1872, it struck a rock off Michipicoten Island and stuck hard. For two days the *Manitoba* remained on the rock until the *Cumberland* of the Collingwood Line came along, took off 75 passengers, and pulled the distressed vessel off. It had to be beached and it sank in 12 feet of water. By July 27, the *Manitoba* had been raised and towed to Detroit for repairs.

On August 26, 1875, the *Manitoba* sank an American propeller-driven steamboat in a collision seven miles southeast of Whitefish Point. The *Manitoba* stopped and rescued ten survivors, including Captain Dugot, but 11 men were lost.

The Carmona, *formerly the Manitoba, c. 1890. Ontario Archives.*

Manitoba, *Fort William, August 16, 1873. Thunder Bay Historical Museum Society.*

In 1888 the *Manitoba* was sold to the Northwest Trading Company of Sarnia which renamed it the *Carmona*. As the *Carmona*, it ran for four years from Sault Ste. Marie to Windsor. In 1898 the general manager of the Windsor, Detroit and Soo Lines announced that, as the *Cambria* had been sold, the route of the *Carmona* had been changed to run from Mackinac Island and Collingwood to the North Channel Island. In the 1890s it operated from Toronto to Lorne and Grimsby Parks, and in 1898, from Kingston to Toronto by the Thousand Island route.

In Collingwood, in 1900, the hull was enlarged to 221 feet long by its new owners, Brown and Company of St. Catharines. It was renamed the *Pittsburgh* and run on the Detroit River. It burned to the water line at the Sandwich Dock near Windsor on August 13, 1903.

The *Cambria* was built in Lévis, Québec, in 1877, as a passenger tug under the name *Champion II*. It was the second of three similar tugs built in the Lévis shipyards: 131 feet long, with a 23-foot beam and an 11-foot draught.

In 1887 the *Champion II* was taken to Owen Sound and rebuilt as the *Cambria*, a passenger ship. It was lengthened to 175 feet. However, when completed, it was found that with the extra weight, the vessel could not maintain an even keel. False sides had to be constructed onto the hull so that it would sit upright.

The *Cambria* was operated on the Owen Sound, North Shore and Sault Ste. Marie route, teamed with the *Carmona*. Both side-wheelers belonged at that time to the Canada Transit Company Limited. Their rivalry was of the keenest, a constant battle for passengers

and freight. The *Carmona* was the speedier of the two and at every chance, it would race with either the *Cambria* or the *Pacific,* which, in those days, was running out of Collingwood. During the race, flames could be seen coming out of the smokestacks, much to the alarm of the passengers.

In the spring of 1891, the steamers were sold. The *Cambria* went to Port Arthur and the *Carmona* to Toronto to operate between Toronto and Port Charlotte, near Niagara. The *Cambria* lost money on the Port Arthur, Duluth run so in September, 1893, the company was satisfied to have a new captain operate it from Windsor to Sault Ste. Marie. Business on this run in 1894 was excellent: a first-class ticket from Windsor to Sault Ste. Marie, return, with meals and berth, was only $15.

The *Cambria* ploughed into a drifting raft of telephone poles on Lake Huron one night in July, 1897, and the disabled hulk was blown

Cambria, *Collingwood, c. 1890. Ontario Archives.*

onto the beach near Point Edward. Mr. Russell Brown of Port Arthur, a survivor, states that two life boats were launched and the passengers put ashore and that he went in the first boat to take crew members. Just as George Ellis, the porter, dropped from the deck into a life boat, the back wash pushed the life boat under the guard of the ship and Ellis dropped into the lake and drowned.

Later in the day, Brown went back to the wreck and got a beautiful silver tankard which had been engraved and presented to the steamer by the citizens of Owen Sound.

The *Cambria* was purchased by a Kingston wrecking company, rebuilt and operated on the Kingston to Toronto passenger and freight route. In 1902 it was scrapped in the area of the old Welland Canal.

The Prairies, the Yukon and the Northwest Territories

Over two thousand square miles of central Canada and the northern United States were carved into interconnecting waterways by retreating glaciers 10,000 years ago. The ice age also resulted in the formation of a gigantic lake, Lake Agassiz, which evolved into present-day Lake Winnipeg. The original expanse of water subsided by evaporation and retreated with the movement of land masses that redistributed drainage and watershed areas.

Except in the central plains, this region of North America is dominated by irregularly coursing small streams. The alluvial soil left by Lake Agassiz is very fertile, producing grasses, flowers and herbs in profusion. The richness of this area made it an excellent environment for fur bearing animals such as the mink, beaver, fox, rabbit and buffalo, and led to the pre-eminence of the fur trade in the Prairies.

The river systems of Alberta, Saskatchewan and Manitoba begin as drainage rivers from the Rocky Mountains. To the south, the Red Deer River, the Bow River and the Oldman River flow east to form the South Saskatchewan River. This in turn flows into the North Saskatchewan River, and empties into Lake Winnipeg.

The Qu'Appelle River flows east to the Assiniboine which meets the Red River at Winnipeg. The Red River then carries their waters south into the central United States.

The northern parts of the Prairie Provinces are drained by the Athabasca and Peace rivers. The Churchill and Nelson rivers empty into Hudson Bay. The Liard River flows through the Northwest Territories. The Skeena and Stikine rivers run into the northwestern section of British Columbia, and eventually into the Yukon River. The Yukon also flows through the American state of Alaska, emptying into the sea at the old Russian port of St.

Michaels. This river was the favourite route for those travelling to the western gold fields. The voyage by steamboat started at St. Michaels. The alternative overland route was through the Chilcoot Pass.

Probably because of their violent glacial origin and the mixture of sedimentary strata that was its result, these rivers have many rocky rapids, sharp turns and shallow areas. One of the most dramatic rapids is the Grand Rapids, where the Saskatchewan River meets Lake Winnipeg. Here the swift water drops nearly one hundred feet, as it travels over a jagged three-mile river bed. The Saskatchewan, like all Prairie rivers, carries a relatively small volume of water along its great length. Its depth was barely sufficient even for the light draught boats of the early river captains, except after heavy rains or a spring thaw. This seasonal variation in the water level also made navigation unpredictable. Nonetheless, here as elsewhere, travel by river was preferable to the tedium and discomfort of a long journey by road.

The interruption of the rivers by frequent shallows, waterfalls and rapids made it impossible for any boat as large as those which plied the Great Lakes to go from one end of a Prairie river system to the other. Freight boats were limited to certain parts of specific rivers, and freight often had to be portaged or transshipped by ox-cart between them. And of course even this limited passage was only possible during the short Prairie summer.

The Hudson's Bay Company received a monopoly in 1757 to trade in furs throughout all the land drained by rivers flowing to Hudson Bay. In practice, the Company took its charter to mean that it could control all the land upon which it built its forts and outposts. It was because of the Hudson's Bay

Company that the rivers of central Canada became important.

Early in the development of the fur trade, the Company had transported its cargo by way of the Ottawa River route. However, the American commercial giants to the south quickly found that the Red River was the best inroad to Canada's fur country. Soon more trading was being done down the Red River into the United States than in Canada.

With the American traders came the paddlewheel steamboats, already a common sight on American rivers. The first steamboat up the Red River to Fort Garry, the *Anson Northrup*, arrived on June 10, 1859. The American traders now had a better, more efficient means of transportation than the York boats used by the Hudson's Bay Company.

The Company realized that its interests, previously protected by isolation, were now defenceless against the hordes of American traders. To protect itself, the Hudson's Bay Company bought the *Anson Northrup* and so gained control of the only steamboat on the Red River. The boat was rebuilt and named the *Pioneer*.

Once steamboats had been established on the Red River, the next step was to extend their use on Lake Winnipeg, and up the Saskatchewan. There was increasing settlement along the Saskatchewan River, and a corresponding increase in trade potential. Moreover the Hudson's Bay Company found it difficult to recruit crews willing to take York boats up the rivers of the Canadian Northwest.

Previous Page:

The sternwheeler Selkirk *at Dufferin, Manitoba, on the Red River, spring 1873. Public Archives of Canada, C 79634.*

Most of the Hudson's Bay Company's trade was still down the Red River to St. Paul, Minnesota. Here it formed an alliance with the Kittson Trading Company. Mr. Kittson became the American representative of the Hudson's Bay Company, and a very senior business partner. Soon he had established a monopoly in steamboats which vanquished all Canadian ventures. The most important of his rivals was the Merchants International Steamboat Line, incorporated in 1875. A Winnipeg concern, this company was denied navigation rights in American waters, and so could not fight Kittson on his own terms. Nonetheless they forged ahead, and in May their enormous new paddlewheeler, the *Manitoba* set a new speed record: from Moorhead to Winnipeg in forty-five hours. They then brought out a sister ship, the *Minnesota*. A price war was on.

Eventually Kittson succeeded in ousting the Merchants International, after various suspicious events which included the ramming — and subsequent sinking — of the *Manitoba* by his ship, the *International*. Kittson was known for unsavoury practices and was later instrumental in the false imprisonment of Louis Riel, who had tried to stop Kittson's employees from distributing liquor to the Indians in Montana.

The *International* began life as an American square-bowed steamer, the *Freighter,* which worked on the Mississippi and Minnesota rivers. In 1859 it was transported overland by John P. Davis and put into the Red River near St. Paul, Minnesota. He wished to win a $3,000 prize offered by a group of American businessmen for the first steamboat to run between St. Paul and Fort Garry. However,

the *Freighter* got stuck on a sand bar and the attempt was abandoned.

In the spring of 1862, the *Pioneer*, formerly the *Anson Northrup,* was crushed by ice and that same spring, the *Freighter* was rebuilt by a Hudson's Bay Company associate. It was 137 feet long, 26 feet wide and had a draught of 40 inches. Two boilers each drove a piston connected to the back paddle wheel. It would burn from 20 to 25 cords a day, stopping along a river bank to load fuel, then docking during the dark hours to be ready for an early start when the sun came up.

The new steamer was launched on the Red River as the *International* on May 20, 1862, at Georgetown, Minnesota, arriving at Fort Garry with a load of Canadian gold prospectors six days later.

The *International,* for many years, was the

The sternwheeler International *on the Assiniboine River in front of Hudson's Bay warehouse with the tower and walls of Fort Garry in the background. On the shore behind the* International *is an empty freight scow. Library, Hudson's Bay Company.*

only boat in the Red River, carrying freight and passengers for the Hudson's Bay Company from the northern United States to Fort Garry. Although it could carry heavy loads, the bulk of freight and manufactured goods still arrived by Red River ox cart which, although slower, could travel a longer season than the *International.*

On the return trip it would bring raw materials, such as animal furs and buffalo hides, to be processed in the commercial centres of the United States. In 1862 it was abandoned for a time at Fort Abercrombe because of the danger of Sioux warfare.

The *International* is noted for the distinguished passengers it carried to and from Fort Garry.

In the early spring of 1869, Louis Riel, leader of the Métis people, stood at the railing of the *International*. He had been away eleven years. "It was early morning when I saw my birthplace again; a Sunday before sunrise. It was a beautiful day. I saw my very dear mother, brothers and sisters the same day."

Alexander Begg, a resident of Fort Garry, wrote in his diary, June 17, 1870: "The steamer *International* arrived about 3 o'clock this afternoon. On board were Father Ritchot with two gentlemen from Montréal. It is rumoured that everything has been arranged satisfactorily even to a general amnesty towards everyone. A salute of 21 guns was fired as soon as Père Ritchot arrived and it was ascertained that his mission had been successful. Father Ritchot had returned to Fort Garry after negotiation for the Métis people with Sir John A. Macdonald."

In July 1870, the *International* arrived at Fort Garry from the United States and the captain hurried to the offices of Louis Riel, now president of the Métis nation. He showed Riel a piece of paper which a maid had found in the cabin of a man who had secretly and stealthily jumped off the boat before it landed at Fort Garry. Riel saw that it was a proclamation signed by Colonel Wolseley, Commander of the Red River Expeditionary Force, urging the Métis not to oppose their entry into Fort Garry.

Not until the next day, was the stranger captured. He was Sir William Francis Butler, agent provocateur, sent by Wolseley to spy upon the Provisional Government. Proving his peaceful intentions, Riel assisted in distribut-

ing further copies of the pronouncement and helped Butler to rejoin Wolseley's troops, who were by now advancing on Fort Garry.

In 1871, with the appearance of the *Selkirk*, ownership of the *International* was transferred to Norman Kittson, an American associate of the Hudson's Bay Company, in an effort to take advantage of American customs laws. This resulted in the formation of the Red River Transportation Company controlled by Kittson, Donald Smith, head of the Hudson's Bay Company in Canada and an important figure in the first Métis Uprising, and James Hill. Hill had previously owned the *Selkirk*, running it in opposition to the *International*.

On June 4, 1875, there were only two steamboats travelling on the entire Red River and they collided near the junction of the Stikine and Red rivers. The *International*'s prow hit the side of the *Manitoba* just behind

The Hudson's Bay Company sternwheeler Anson Northrup, c. 1865. Metropolitan Toronto Library Board.

the smokestacks. Within minutes, the *Manitoba* had filled with water and sunk. Within weeks, both boats were again in service.

The *Anson Northrup* was built on the Mississippi River in 1859, and then was dismantled and carried to a tributary of the Red River where it was rebuilt. It was 90 feet long and 22 feet wide. In 1859, it made the first steamboat trip north to Fort Garry; thereafter, it ran regularly, carrying passengers and cargo between St. Paul, Minnesota, and Fort Garry. In 1861 it was bought by the Hudson's Bay Company and was renamed the *Pioneer*. The first Canadian-owned sternwheeler in the Canadian West, it was wrecked in 1862.

The sternwheeler *Manitoba* was built at Moorehead, North Dakota, in 1875. It was all wood, 128 feet long, 31 feet wide and four feet deep. It originally belonged to the Red River Transportation Company which was controlled by an American company, the Kittson Line.

The Kittson Line distributed supplies throughout north central United States. To retain its trading monopolies, it would assist friendly politicians in getting elected. Because of his corruption, Norman W. Kittson made an enemy of Louis Riel, who was then living with the Métis in the United States. Kittson and his agents falsely accused Riel of election irregularities and at a critical stage of the elections, Riel was jailed. Riel was eventually cleared of all charges and continued his campaign to prohibit Kittson from selling liquor to Indians and Métis.

The *Manitoba* had a bad reputation among sailors. In its first three years of service, 1875–8, it had three collisions, a fire, and lost a passenger overboard.

In 1881, the Winnipeg and Western Transportation Company bought the *Manitoba* and rebuilt it at Grand Rapids, Manitoba, adding 50 feet to its length.

During 1883, the *Manitoba*, commanded by Captain James Launderdale, made a trip from Cumberland House to Edmonton, as well as to Prince Albert, Battleford and Fort Pitt.

In the spring of 1885, the *Manitoba* was one of three sternwheelers in the Prince Albert area available to the government to transport troops to quell the second Métis Uprising. The *North West* and the *Marquis* were easily freed from the ice. However, the *Manitoba* remained frozen to the bottom of the Sturgeon River. Later, as the river broke up, ice piled against the *Manitoba* to a height of 20 feet, crushing the steamer beyond repair.

The unlucky Manitoba *is seen here docked at Fisher's Landing, Minnesota in 1877. Public Archives of Canada, C 35876.*

The sidewheeler *Princess* was launched in Winnipeg on August 2, 1881. The *Princess* was 153 feet long, 24 feet wide and eight feet deep. It had two grey funnels, 60 feet high. On its wheel guard were painted golden beavers. It was capable of carrying 600 passengers. The cabin deck was 120 feet long with berths for 75 passengers. The second deck had small private staterooms, two bridal suites and a $5,000 piano.

Later that year, it pulled the hulk of the large steamer *City of Winnipeg* on its way to the Saskatchewan River. They encountered three terrific storms, and the weakened hull of the *City of Winnipeg* began coming apart. If it sank, it would pull the *Princess* down with it. So the ships were cut apart, the *City of Winnipeg* beached itself, and disintegrated.

The North Western Navigation Company operated the *Princess* on the Saskatchewan River system supplying trading posts. In early 1883, the ship was overhauled, repainted and refurnished. It was recorded to have reached Prince Albert on July 1, 1883, with 196 tons of freight and to have run between Grand Rapids and Prince Albert for the remainder of the season.

The *Princess* ran from Fort Garry, across Lake Winnipeg, to Grand Rapids. The freight and passengers were then portaged for about three miles to continue their journey westward on either the *North West*, the *Northcote* or the *Marquis*. By 1885, the *Princess* was the largest Lake Winnipeg steamer still working.

In 1895 the ship was abandoned and towed to Selkirk in 1900. In 1904, the *Princess* was completely rebuilt at the North West Navigation Shipyards at Winnipeg to be a freight boat. The side wheels were removed and replaced with a propeller. In 1906, the *Princess*, while carrying a load of fish, ran full speed onto the beach because the helmsman fell

Princess at Winnipeg, c. 1895. Manitoba Archives.

asleep at the wheel. It was removed, repaired and continued to carry fish to the freezing and storage plants.

On August 25, 1906, the *Princess* sprang a leak which, in the space of one day, overcame the pumps, put out the furnace fires, and left the *Princess* to the mercy of a powerful storm. It drifted onto a reef which broke the boat in half. The boilers fell through the hull, carrying six crew members to their deaths. Most of the passengers and crew drowned. The captain was found drowned on his hands and knees under the wheelhouse.

The waves pounded the rest of the boat to pieces on the shores of Swampy Island.

The *Dakota* was built at Breckenridge, Minnesota, in 1872. It was 92 feet long and 23 feet wide. On its first trip, in 1873, it travelled up the Red River into Canada, past Fort Garry and as far as Dufferin, Manitoba, arriving May 6, 1873. The Red River Transportation Company operated the *Dakota* during 1874 and 1875.

Its usual route was from Fargo, North Dakota, to Fort Garry—always crammed with passengers and freight. Most of the passengers were settlers, taking up their 160 acre allotments of cheap farmland on the prairies. On the return trip, the steamboat would push barges loaded with wheat and buffalo hides.

The *Dakota* accidentally burned at Pembina, Manitoba, in 1881.

Right:
The sternwheeler Dakota *at Dufferin, Manitoba, on the Red River in the spring of 1873. Public Archives of Canada, C 79635.*

The sternwheeler *Marquis* was built in 1882 at Grand Rapids, Manitoba, for the Winnipeg and Western Transportation Company. It was 201 feet long, 34 feet wide and five feet deep.

A description of its engines has come down to us. There were two horizontal high-pressure engines, rated at 83 horsepower, which could drive the vessel 16 miles per hour. Steam was produced by three boilers each generating 125 pounds pressure. Each steam cylinder was 19 inches in diameter; the piston stroke was six feet. The *Marquis* had four rudders in front of the paddle wheel to give it greater manoeuvrability.

The largest and most luxurious of the Saskatchewan steamers, the *Marquis* first operated on Lake Winnipeg on September 25, 1882. It later went up the Saskatchewan River as far as Prince Albert.

On May 8, 1885, the *Marquis* was hired to take part, with the *Northcote*, in the attack on the Métis capital of Batoche. It left Prince Albert with a contingent of North West Mounted Police on board and on May 12, accompanied by the *Northcote*, started for Batoche. However, the *Marquis'* steering gear, previously damaged by ice, broke down again. It was to be towed to Batoche, which had by then fallen to the Canadian Army. The ship was repaired and the *Marquis* was used as a floating headquarters by General Middleton for the remainder of the Métis campaign.

In 1886, the *Marquis*, under the direction of Captain Julius Dougal, on its first trip as a civilian vessel again, carried a record 250 tons of freight and 100,000 feet of lumber for Battleford.

On the next trip, carrying only 97 tons of freight, the *Marquis* entered the dangerous Thorburn Rapids which are a mile in length and have a deceptive six-mile-an-hour flow. When it was almost through the rapids, going

Marquis, *c. 1884. Manitoba Archives.*

against the current, its port side glanced off a rock, causing the bow to swing to the right. Caught by the downward force of the water, the bow was pushed further over, swung broadside into the current, and turned completely around so that it was headed back downstream.

The rock made a hole in the hull under the forward end, near the boilers. Water poured in and, in half an hour, the *Marquis* sank in about four feet of water.

Mr. McArthur, the original builder, attempted to salvage the ship when the river was extremely low. Its 475 tons were jacked up and skids were put under it. Ten sets of tackle were used to slowly pull the vessel up a slipway. However, the ropes broke under the strain,

and the *Marquis* slid backward, crashing once again into the river and the rocks below. This second crash broke its main steam pipes and hog chains, making salvage virtually impossible. Nevertheless, the steamer was once again jacked up to protect it from the ice and left for the fast-approaching winter.

The *Marquis* remained on the jacks and slowly disintegrated. Its wood was used to build a house and its machinery scavenged piece by piece. All that remains is its bell, part of its smokestack, and a gavel made from the wood of its hull, all in the Prince Albert Museum.

The *Selkirk* was launched at McCauleyville, Minnesota, in 1871. It was 108 feet long.

It began running up the Red River from Grand Forks, North Dakota, to Fort Garry in competition to the *International*, both boats doing their utmost to make the trip as fast as possible. However, the *Selkirk* and *International* were both owned by the Red River Navigation Company which now had a monopoly on Red River steamboats. They charged exorbitant rates for their services. On October 8, 1877, the *Selkirk* pushed before it several barges and, on one of these, was the train engine, "Countess of Dufferin," the first locomotive to run in the City of Winnipeg. Our photograph shows the engine being loaded onto one of the barges.

The *Selkirk* was wrecked at Grand Forks, North Dakota, in 1884.

Selkirk *at Moorhead Levee, North Dakota, c. 1877. Manitoba Archives.*

Selkirk *loading the "Countess of Dufferin" on October 19, 1877 at Point Douglas, Winnipeg. Ontario Archives.*

In 1887, [handwritten: 1874] the *Northcote* was built in Grand Rapids, North Dakota. Designed like a Mississippi River steamboat, the first deck was used for cargo and fuel storage, and the second was outfitted with passenger cabins. The sternwheeler was 150 feet long, 28 feet wide and five feet deep. Its engines had been salvaged from another boat and could generate 39 horsepower. There were two tall smokestacks in front of the wheelhouse. Named after Sir Stafford Northcote, Governor of the Hudson's Bay Company, 1869–74, the *Northcote* was launched August 1, 1875. [handwritten: 1874]

The *Northcote* stopped first, that year, at The Pas. It then proceeded 240 miles further to Fort La Corne and 12 days later, reached its final destination, Carlton House, 490 miles up the Saskatchewan River system. It was the first steam vessel to navigate successfully from St. Paul, Minnesota, to Carlton House.

The *Northcote's* route depended on the water level of the Saskatchewan River system as it could not travel certain rapids during periods of low water, despite its very shallow draught. In 1875, the *Northcote* also reached Fort Edmonton with 130 tons of freight. In subsequent years it delivered freight on both the North and South Saskatchewan rivers.

The *Northcote* pioneered a technique called "grasshoppering." Prairie rivers were often blocked by sandbars, the most renowned sandbar being in the area called "The Elbow" on the South Saskatchewan.

If the sandbar was narrow, the sternwheeler might approach it at full speed. Hopefully, it would have enough momentum to slide the hull over the other side.

However larger sandbars required other forms of attack. The boat might be turned around so that the thrashing paddle wheel stirred the water, chewing up the sandbar and washing it away.

But it was for the wider, higher sandbars that "grasshoppering" was used. Two very large poles or spars were usually carried on the front of the boat and used as booms for loading heavy freight. The spars were placed in the sand at an angle, inclined forward, about 15 yards in front of the boat. Ropes were attached from the hull to the pulley at the far end of the spar then back to the capstan on the deck. The donkey engine was fired up to turn the capstan. The vessel would thus pull itself forward over the sandbar a few yards at a time.

Around 1880, the *Northcote* was modified to provide accommodation for 50 passengers. In 1881 it transported the Marquis of Lorne and his entourage on part of their trip to western Canada.

In 1882 the Hudson's Bay Company sold out its interest in the *Northcote* but the ship continued to run on the Saskatchewan River system.

The *Northcote* was to fight and lose Canada's first naval battle. In 1885 the *Northcote* was leased by the Canadian Government to assist in its campaign against the Second Métis Uprising. The vessel was in charge of Captains Seegers and Sheets. The home and barn of Gabriel Dumont, the Métis general, were dismantled and the stout boards nailed for protection around the sides of the *Northcote*.

General George Middleton, the leader of the Canadian forces, had planned to use the *Northcote* in his attack on the Métis capital of Batoche, Saskatchewan. However, due to communication difficulties, the *Northcote* attacked too early and all alone.

Métis snipers, along the South Saskatchewan River bank, poured bullets into the pilot house, endeavouring to kill the helmsman. In order to escape this barrage of hot lead, he lay down on the floor on his back and steered with his feet, peering through a crack in the boards and listening to frantic shouts from the soldiers on deck.

As the *Northcote* came opposite Batoche, the Métis, attempting to entrap the boat, lowered the heavy ferry cable which was stretched across the river. They miscalculated. They were too late, ensnaring only the smokestacks, which were easily torn off.

The furnaces were under forced draft. Intense heat, smoke, cinders and burning wood particles poured out of the smokestack stumps onto the vessel, blinding the helmsman and setting the decks on fire. Unable to see, the helmsman headed the steamer into the river bank and probable captivity.

Captain Seegers rang the engineer to reverse the engines. However, there was no one in the engine room, as the engineer, frightened by the hail of gunfire, had run to the safety of the hold. The fireman, Dan Herce, ran back to the engine room and reversed the engines, keeping the vessel in midstream.

The *Northcote* now attempted to flee the sharpshooters, bumping its way along the banks of the river. The crew put out the fires on deck but refused to return to battle. Afterwards, they counted 90 bullet holes in the walls of the wheelhouse.

Later, the *Northcote* transported wounded soldiers and Louis Riel, on his way to his destiny in Regina.

In 1886, the *Northcote* was abandoned, beached at Cumberland House, and slowly disintegrated.

Sternwheeler Northcote *and the smaller* Minnow, *protected by Gabriel Dumont's barn-boards at Batoche, 1885. Public Archives of Canada, C 3448.*

Bottom:
Northcote *unloading supplies at Batoche, 1885. Public Archives of Canada, C 3447.*

Bottom Right:
Northcote *beached at Cumberland House, c. 1894. Manitoba Archives.*

A sedate and beautiful sternwheeler, the *North West* was built in Moorehead, North Dakota, in 1881, for service up the Red River into Canada. It was 200 feet long, 38 feet wide and five feet deep. The *North West* was powered by an engine with two 16-inch cylinders, each with a five-foot stroke. Steam was generated in two steel boilers, each having ten flues.

The main cabin was 120 feet long and there were berths for 80 passengers. The salon contained the first piano on a Northwest river boat. The second deck was a spacious ten feet above the first, and the hurricane deck was eight feet above that. The cost was $27,000.

The *North West* was owned by Peter McArthur. On March 15, 1882, he sold it to the North West Transportation Company which in turn sold it on April 16, 1884, to the Winnipeg and Western Transportation Company. It was put under the command of Captain James Sheets.

In the spring of 1882, the *North West* made a perilous crossing of Lake Winnipeg to Grand Rapids, Manitoba. So bad were the storms this season that the sailors filled the holds with empty watertight coal oil barrels so that if the ship took on too much water it would still, perhaps, stay afloat.

Arriving at Grand Rapids, the *North West* did not have enough power to ascend these turbulent waters at the mouth of the Saskatchewan River. However, on July 4, 1882, it was able to begin the ascent with the assistance of a half-mile-long rope, tied to one large tree after another. The other end of the rope was tied onto the capstan on the bow. A donkey engine wound the rope around the capstan, pulling the boat forward.

The next day, with the paddle wheel thrashing the turbulent waters and the donkey engine turning the capstan, the *North West* travelled a further mile before the capstan

broke. On July 6, the paddle wheel was damaged. On July 7, the capstan broke again, but by now, the *North West* was close enough to the end of the rapids that the *Northcote* was able to help.

The *Northcote* tied itself to the shore and tied a second line, almost half a mile long, from the *North West* to its own capstan. Then, with the paddle of the *North West* beating the waters, and the donkey engines of each boat revolving their capstans, the struggling sternwheeler was pulled further up the rapids.

Hudson's Bay Company sternwheeler North West *at Edmonton, 1896. E. Brown Collection, Alberta Archives.*

As it passed over the last rocks, the *North West* became stuck in midstream. All power was applied to all engines, and a final, mighty pull set the *North West* free. The hog chains snapped and the boat almost broke into pieces, but the main chain held and the *North West* was safe.

The *North West* immediately began loading freight for ports on the Saskatchewan River system. It called at The Pas, Battleford, Fort La Corne, Prince Albert, Carlton House and Edmonton. It was to continue on this route for many years, suffering numerous accidents as it ran the many rapids of the system.

During the Métis Uprising of 1885, the *North West* was used to transport troops and military equipment in the areas of Prince Albert and Batoche.

One of its most serious accidents occurred in 1886, at a spot 50 miles below Edmonton. When the vessel entered shallow water, the pilot rang for slow speed, but the engineer put the engines onto full power, driving the *North West* up onto the rocky shoals. The bow and stern ended up lower than the centre, which was humped up. The force was so great it broke the bracing hog chains and their supporting rods. Again the main chain held. Repairs took a few days and required the setting up of a temporary blacksmith shop. The *North West* limped into Prince Albert for further repairs.

It was beached between 1886 and 1888. Its last voyage started August 7, 1899, when it broke loose from its moorings in the swollen North Saskatchewan River, struck some submerged piles, and began to take on water. The *North West* drifted downriver with no-one on board, and sank. It was scrapped in Edmonton in 1903.

David N. Winton, *Saskatchewan River, The Pas, Manitoba, c. 1950. Public Archives, PA 14005.*

George V *was wrecked by the spring ice at The Pas, Manitoba, in 1919. The engine was salvaged and installed in the* David N. Winton. *Saskatchewan Archives.*

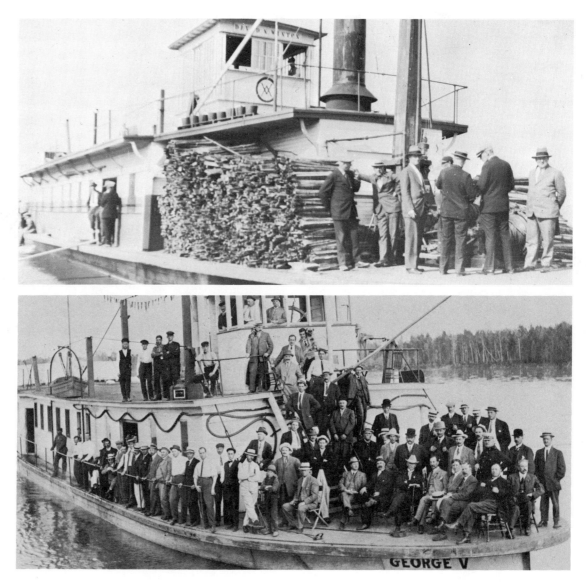

The diminutive sternwheeler *David N. Winton* was built at The Pas, Manitoba, in 1920. It was 120 feet long and 25 feet wide. Its engines came from the sternwheeler *George V* which was destroyed by ice in 1919. The *David N. Winton* carried freight on the Saskatchewan River system, but was later moved to the Carrot River District where it towed log booms for the rest of its days. In the spring of 1954, ice jams wrecked and sunk the faithful *David N. Winton.*

The ill-fated sternwheeler *City of Medicine Hat* was built in Medicine Hat, Alberta, in 1907. It was 120 feet long, 25 feet wide and only two feet deep. The engines could produce 125 horsepower. The sternwheeler was commanded by Captain H. H. Ross who operated boats out of Medicine Hat and The Pas. His first command was the *Assiniboia*, but it was destroyed by ice at Cedar Lake in 1906.

The *Daily Phoenix* of Medicine Hat reported that on June 6, 1908, a cruise of the *City of Medicine Hat* had come to an abrupt and disastrous end when it was dashed against a concrete bridge pier by the powerful currents in the South Saskatchewan River in Saskatoon. The steamer swung around in the strong current and struck a second concrete pier, coming to rest up against it on its port side. The hull partly filled with water and lay at an angle of about 75 degrees.

Captain Ross and his crew scrambled for safety but not without a terrifying few minutes and a narrow escape. Those on board lost practically everything they had. However, as the ship lay on its side, the crew went back in and pulled out several loads of silk furnishings which were being hauled into Medicine Hat.

While the ship was pitching against the bridge, the barge it was towing tipped over and scattered about $500 worth of coal along the river bed. The barge was later caught and tied up about a quarter-mile below. A group of cowboys arrived at the east end of the bridge, just as the mishap occurred, with a big herd of cattle. Half of the herd were forced through the crowd watching the wreck. Happily, no one was injured.

The *City of Medicine Hat* was never salvaged and, over the years, slowly disintegrated.

City of Medicine Hat. *Public Archives of Canada, PA 37865.*

The wreck of the City of Medicine Hat, *June 7, 1908. The greatest marine disaster in the history of Saskatoon, Saskatchewan. Public Archives of Canada, PA 38502.*

The sternwheeler *Alberta* was built in Medicine Hat in 1884. Owned by Coates and Mosher's, it was 100 feet long, 20 feet wide and three feet deep, with two 30-horse power engines. It was named in honour of her Royal Highness Princess Louise Caroline Alberta, wife of the Marquis of Lorne, the Governor-General of Canada. Our picture shows it docked at Rat Portage.

During the Métis Uprising of 1885, the *Alberta* was used to transport government troops, ammunition and arms. On July 5, 1885, it was transformed into a hospital ship, taking the wounded from Prince Albert. It also towed barges containing fuel, supplies, cattle and wounded soldiers to Regina. As river traffic had decreased, the *Alberta* was beached in 1886 and scrapped in 1887.

The Alberta. *Saskatchewan Archives.*

Alberta. *Public Archives of Canada, PA 11644.*

The *Athabasca*, the first of three steamers to
bear this name, was one of the earliest ships in
the North. It was built by the Hudson's Bay
Company at Athabasca Landing, Alberta, in
1888, to service the Lesser Slave Lake area. It
was 146 feet long, 28 feet wide, and four feet
deep. Because it had to travel in such shallow
water, it was equipped with spars to get it over
sandbars.

On its first trip in August, 1888, the *Athabasca* was unable to make it to Lesser Slave
Lake. After it had gone only a short distance
on the Lesser Slave Lake River, it hit a rock
and sank in 14 inches of water. After much
repairing and pumping of water, the new
steamer returned to Athabasca Landing with
Captain John Scribner Segers in disgrace.

The water in the river was not high enough
until June, 1892, to enable the *Athabasca* to
steam into Lesser Slave Lake. However, the
lake was blocked with ice, forcing the ship to
return to Athabasca Landing. It did finally
succeed the next year. The *Athabasca* operated
for many years throughout the area carrying,
among other things, Klondike gold seekers.

The steamer was condemned in 1903. In
1920, the engines, machinery and passenger
accommodation were removed and the *Athabasca* was rebuilt as a scow.

Athabasca *about to be drawn up onto the river
bank before the winter freeze up. E. Brown
Collection, Alberta Archives.*

Facing Page:
Hudson's Bay Company sternwheeler, the
Athabasca, *at the head of Grand Rapids in the
Athabasca River in 1893. Public Archives of
Canada, PA 45370.*

The Hudson's Bay Company built two boats named *Athabasca River*. The first was built at Athabasca Landing, Alberta, in 1912. The second, the vessel in our photograph, was built at Fort McMurray in 1922 for operation between Fort McMurray and Fort Fitzgerald. Its length was 148 feet with a 36-foot beam and a six-foot depth; its tonnage was registered at 860. The *Athabasca River* was in operation until the fall of 1946.

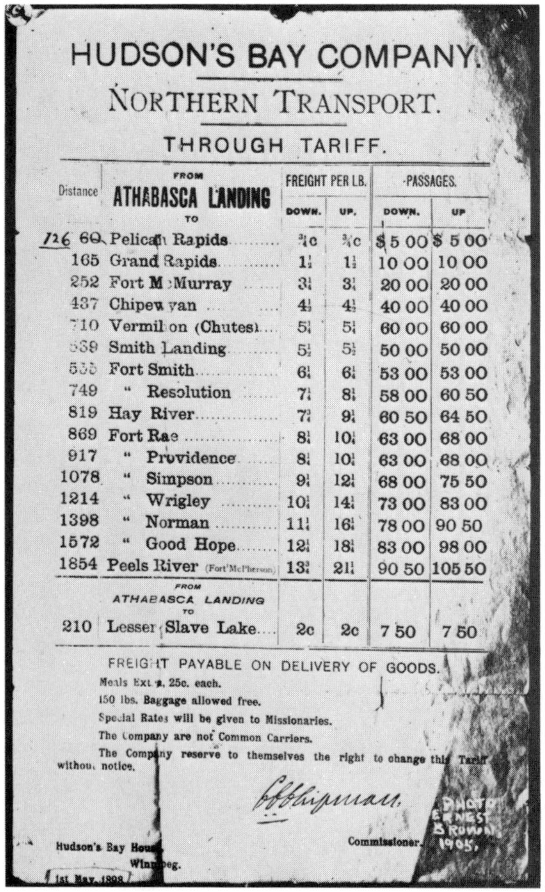

HUDSON'S BAY COMPANY.

NORTHERN TRANSPORT.

THROUGH TARIFF.

Distance	FROM ATHABASCA LANDING TO	FREIGHT PER LB.		PASSAGES.	
		DOWN.	UP.	DOWN.	UP
126 60	Pelican Rapids	¾c	¾c	$5 00	$5 00
165	Grand Rapids	1½	1½	10 00	10 00
252	Fort McMurray	3¼	3¼	20 00	20 00
437	Chipewyan	4½	4½	40 00	40 00
710	Vermilion (Chutes)	5¼	5¼	60 00	60 00
539	Smith Landing	5½	5½	50 00	50 00
555	Fort Smith	6¼	6¼	53 00	53 00
749	" Resolution	7¼	8¼	58 00	60 50
819	Hay River	7¾	9¼	60 50	64 50
869	Fort Rae	8¼	10¼	63 00	68 00
917	" Providence	8¼	10¼	63 00	68 00
1078	" Simpson	9¼	12¼	68 00	75 50
1214	" Wrigley	10¼	14¼	73 00	83 00
1398	" Norman	11¼	16¼	78 00	90 50
1572	" Good Hope	12¼	18¼	83 00	98 00
1854	Peels River (Fort McPherson)	13¾	21¼	90 50	105 50
	FROM ATHABASCA LANDING TO				
210	Lesser Slave Lake	2c	2c	7 50	7 50

FREIGHT PAYABLE ON DELIVERY OF GOODS.

Meals Extra, 25c. each.

150 lbs. Baggage allowed free.

Special Rates will be given to Missionaries.

The Company are not Common Carriers.

The Company reserve to themselves the right to change this Tariff without notice.

C. C. Chipman.
Commissioner.

Hudson's Bay House,
Winnipeg.
1st May, 1898.

PHOTO ERNEST BROWN 1905.

The Hudson's Bay Company rates for the Athabasca River *in 1898. Departure and arrival times are not noted because they were most uncertain. Public Archives of Canada, C 7168.*

The Athabasca River, *discharging freight for the Hudson's Bay Company on the Athabasca River near Fort McMurray. Hudson's Bay Company Library.*

On July 8, 1882, the *Northcote* arrived at Edmonton with 25,000 pounds of material to be used in constructing a sternwheeler at Fort Chipewyan on Lake Athabasca, to be named after Commissioner Grahame of the Hudson's Bay Company. Under the direction of the construction engineer, J. Littlebury, it was moved, using nine wagons and 31 carts, to Athabasca Landing. It was then towed on scows over the Grand Rapids to Fort McMurray and the safer waters of Lake Athabasca to Fort Chipewyan.

During the summer, Captain John H. Smith arrived and began construction of the *Grahame*, which was to be 130 feet long, 24 feet wide and four feet deep. It was designed to carry 200 tons of freight. By November 10, 1883, the sternwheeler was assembled, in the water, and Captain Smith was back in Edmonton having completed his testing.

On June 15, 1885, the *Grahame* made its first commercial run. With sparks flying (from the burning green cordwood in her furnaces), it covered 120 miles to Grahame's Landing in seven and one-half hours. It took 15 hours, fighting against the current, to return.

The next trip was up to Fort McMurray, and this was accomplished in 15 hours. Coming back against the current took 30 hours. From then on, the *Grahame* was the pride and wonder of Lake Athabasca. To ride on it was an adventure to be recalled with the passing years.

On its route, the *Grahame* passed the Athabasca Tar Sands. This provided the opportunity for the engineers to throw chunks of the tar into the furnace of the *Grahame* to heat it up once the fire was started.

During 1897–98, the *Grahame* transported over 700 prospectors on their way to the Klondike gold fields. By 1904, it was making regular trips between Fort McMurray and

Smiths Landing, often transporting cattle. One of the passengers wrote that when they ran out of fodder, the captain used the hay from the mattresses to feet his hungry freight animals.

A few years later, the *Grahame* was transporting disillusioned gold seekers back home. By 1911, the *Grahame* was still running its summer schedule, but most freight was going by train and the steamboats only serviced the smaller riverside communities. By 1914 the *Grahame* had been beached and its engines were removed in 1921 to provide power for the new Hudson's Bay sternwheeler, the *Athabasca River*.

The Hudson's Bay Company sternwheeler Grahame I, *at Fort Chipewyan, Alberta, 1893. Public Archives of Canada, PA 45360.*

The famous old sternwheeler, *D. A. Thomas,* was built at Peace River Crossing, Alberta, in 1916. It was 162 feet long, 37 feet wide, with a six-foot draught.

The Hudson's Bay Company needed the steamer on the Fort McMurray-Fitzgerald route. To get there, the sternwheeler had to go over the Vermillion Chutes on the Peace River. This involved floating a 114-ton vessel over a 30-foot waterfall. To compound the problem, it had to pass through a channel approximately 50 feet wide. This meant that as the Captain was shooting the 30-foot falls, he had about five feet clearance on each side.

Under Captain Cowley and pilot Louis Bourassa, the sternwheeler approached the waterfall, started over the lip and grounded, stuck tight just at the top of the falls. Because the *D. A. Thomas* filled the river bed, the water piled up behind it, raising the stern high enough to tip the ship over the rocky ledge. It was pushed over the falls into the whirlpool below. The bow bounced upwards, pulling the back of the boat over the rock ledge, breaking part of the backpaddle. But the massive boat now floated free, below the Vermilion Chutes.

After years of faithful service, the *D. A. Thomas* was wrecked near Dunvegan, B.C., in 1929.

D.A. Thomas *on the Peace River, c. 1920.*
Public Archives of Canada, PA 45141.

The *Portus B. Weare* was a typical Yukon River flat-bottomed sternwheeler, three decks high, with two smokestacks behind the wheelhouse.

The bow and stern were flat and on a level with the bank, when moored. The first deck was enclosed and used mainly for freight and passengers who had very little money, ate their own food, and slept in their own sleeping bags. The second deck contained a few private cabins and a large dormitory area. Around its walls were bunks and in its centre sat a wood-burning stove for heating, cooking and drying wet, smelly clothes. The third, or top deck, contained the Captain's quarters and the wheelhouse. The steamer was painted white when the season began but was a sooty, grey, banged-up mess by the time winter came.

After leaving the Port of St. Michaels, there were about 80 miles of open sea before the steamer entered the mouth of the Yukon River. This trip could only be made in fine weather because the steamers were unstable in rough weather. During the passage, the boilers and the steam engine used salt water. When the boat reached the fresh water of the Yukon River, it had to stop. All the salt water had to be pumped out of the engine by hand and fresh water pumped in again. The heat and the salt would otherwise rust the engine parts very quickly. This would often take the crew and its passengers a whole day. Only then could the boat begin its journey up the River.

The trip was generally speaking very monotonous with nothing for the men to do but sit on their bunks. The only way one could get any exercise was when they stopped to "wood up." Then there were clouds of mosquitoes and blackflies.

The dormitory in the second deck became stiflingly hot when the windows were closed because the heat from the boilers on the first

The Portus B. Weare, *Authors Private Collection.*

deck rose and was trapped in the second deck. The passengers soon referred to their boat as a "flat-bottomed, wood-burning, stew pan."

The men made many references to eating, as their food also was monotonous. The three meals were generally salt pork and potatoes and, occasionally, smoked bacon and pea soup. It was impossible to carry or buy fresh food along the way. Any edible animal was quickly shot, hoisted on board, and eaten. Moose abounded and, for a few days, every meal would be a variation of boiled, fried, stewed, and reheated moosemeat.

The *Portus B. Weare* burned wood, which had to be collected at frequent intervals during the journey. Passengers and crew both went ashore, armed with axes, and set to work chopping enough wood to take them a few more miles up the river. When the current was very swift, this boat would burn a cord-and-a-half to two cords of wood per hour. The steamboat was able to travel about 80 miles a day against the current.

There were portions of the Yukon River which were so shallow that the steamer would have to turn around and use its paddle wheel to dig the soft sand out of the river bottom in order to give itself enough draught. Very often, the passengers and the crew had to disembark to lighten the steamer so it could proceed through the shallows.

Because of these shallows, only relatively small steamboats were able to navigate the Yukon Rivers and these boats were powered by small engines. During periods of high water, the current in the Yukon River could become very swift. It was not too unusual to have the steamboat engine driving the paddles at full speed and the boat actually drifting backwards.

The 1,800-mile trip up the Yukon to Forty Mile River took 19 days. The Klondike goldfields were still 50 miles further up, which were navigable only by very small boats.

Today four sternwheelers can be seen intact in the Yukon: the *Klondike* and *Aksala* in Whitehorse; the *Tutshi* in Carcross; and the *Keno* in Dawson City. Two others, the *Casca* and the *Whitehorse*, which were beached on the banks of the Yukon River at Whitehorse, accidentally burned to the ground in June, 1974.

There were two sternwheelers on the Yukon River named *Klondike*. The *Klondike I* was launched in 1929 by the British Yukon Navigation Company. It was a new design which allowed a 50% increase in cargo capacity without sacrificing its shallow draught. It carried so much freight that it did not have to push a barge to attain a payload. It travelled a regular route on the Yukon River until 1936 when it struck a reef and broke its back.

The present *Klondike* was built in 1937, using the machinery and boiler from the wrecked vessel. The boiler had originally come from another old steamer, the *Yukoner*, which had been retired for many years in Whitehorse. The *Klondike II* is 210 feet long, with a 42-foot beam, and a draught of six feet.

For years it was used between Whitehorse and Dawson City as freighter, as it had very little passenger accommodation. In 1945, extra staterooms were added and in 1953, a bar and lounge. When travelling with the current, the run took only 36 hours, but going upstream, the trip took five days. When all-weather roads were constructed along the Klondike, in 1950, the sternwheelers were no longer economical for freight transport.

The *Klondike* continued in operation until 1955. Now resting on the north bank of the Yukon River, in Whitehorse, the *Klondike* is to become a National Historic Site. It is open during the summer months and guided tours are made available by Parks Canada.

The Klondike II *at Whitehorse on the Yukon River, c. 1960. Yukon Territory Tourism and Information Branch.*

The wreck of the Klondike I. *Public Archives of Canada, C 25195.*

The *Tutshi,* pronounced "Too-shy," was built for the British Yukon Navigation Company at Carcross, Yukon Territory, in 1917, to carry freight and passengers on the Yukon River and Lake Tagish. It was 167 feet long, 35 feet wide and had a draught of six feet. It was withdrawn from service in 1954, and a year later, drawn up on the shore near the railway station, where it had been built. It can be seen today on display along with the first steam locomotive engine in the northwest, the "Duchess."

The Tutshi, *with a mail buggy and the engine "Duchess," on display on the bank of the Yukon River at Carcross, Yukon Territory. Yukon Territory Tourism and Information Branch.*

The Tutshi *arriving at Carcross, ready to be drawn up on the Yukon River bank for display. British Columbia Archives.*

The *Aksala,* weighing 642 tons, was first named the *Alaska,* and built by the Alaska Yukon Navigation Company in Whitehorse in 1913. It is 167 feet long, 35 feet wide and six feet deep. It was transferred to Canadian registry and renamed *Aksala.* It was laid up in 1955 and may now be seen at Mile 913 on the Alaska Highway near Whitehorse.

The *Keno* began life at Whitehorse, Yukon, in 1922. Its hull was 131 feet long, 29 feet wide and five feet deep. It was built for the British Yukon Navigation Company for service in the Upper Yukon River. In April, 1933, its captain, John D. Murray, died while in command on the Stewart River. The *Keno* was completely rebuilt at Whitehorse in 1937, and lengthened to 141 feet.

The *Keno* was the last sternwheeler to travel the Yukon River. On August 26, 1960, commanded by F. S. Blakely, it made its last trip from Whitehorse to Dawson City, arriving on the 29th.

It was beached in downtown Dawson City, restored and turned into a museum. The gangway swings out on to Front Street to welcome visitors on board throughout the summer.

The Keno *at Dawson City, Yukon Territory.*
Yukon Territory Tourism and Information Branch.

This beautiful sternwheeler, the *Whitehorse*, was built in Whitehorse, in 1901. Its hull was 167 feet long, 35 feet wide, five feet deep. Known to old-time steamboat men as "The Old Gray Mare," it faithfully steamed the Yukon River until it had to be rebuilt at Whitehorse in 1930. It served another 25 years until 1955, when it was beached beside the *Casca* at Dawson City. Local citizens considered the two old steamers an eyesore. They came to a fiery end. In 1974, they were accidentally burned to the ground.

The first *Casca* was built in Victoria in 1898. The hull was 140 feet long, 31 feet wide and five feet deep. Under its own power, it made the dangerous ocean voyage north to St. Michaels and to the Yukon River and Dawson City.

It was rebuilt at Whitehorse and lengthened 20 feet in 1912 for the British Yukon Navigation Company. They ran it until 1936 when it was drawn up on the bank of the Yukon River at Dawson City. Here it rested beside the *Whitehorse* until they were both destroyed by fire in June, 1974.

A second *Casca* was wrecked July 9, 1936, in Rink Rapids on the Yukon River. It was a total loss except for machinery. *Casca III,* 1,300 tons, was built in Whitehorse in 1936 by the British Yukon Navigation Company, the river division of the White Pass and Yukon Route, which still operates railroad and truck lines in the Territory.

The Casca *and the* Whitehorse *on the banks of the Yukon River at Dawson City before they were both destroyed by fire in June, 1974. Yukon Territory Tourism and Information Branch.*

The *Nasutlin* was built in Whitehorse, Yukon Territory, in 1912. It was 115 feet long, 27 feet wide and four feet deep. In the fall of 1919, it was trapped in the ice above Mayo on the Yukon River. The next spring it was damaged by the ice and sank May 24, 1920.

The Nasutlin, *Public Archives of Canada, C 4310.*

The *Wrigley* is the first of two boats built by the Hudson's Bay Company in 1886, and 1898 at Fort Smith, N.W.T., and named the *Wrigley* after Joseph Wrigley, the president of the Winnipeg and Western Transportation Company.

In mid-summer of 1885, Captain Smith of the *Grahame*, towed two scow-loads of equipment down the Mackenzie to Fort Smith for the building of the first *Wrigley*. On one of the scows were two large boilers. However, the scow was wrecked when it hit a stretch of rapids, and one of the boilers dropped out of sight in the deep water. From then on, these rapids were known as Boiler Rapids.

After many weeks, Captain Smith was able to put a line on the underwater boiler, pull it to shore, reload it on a scow and see it safely installed in the *Wrigley*. The *Wrigley I* was 83 feet long, 15 feet wide and seven feet deep and registered at 90 tons. It was built of hand-sawn native green spruce, and because of this, the vessel had a relatively short life.

It was operated by Captain Smith between Fort Smith and Fort MacPherson on the Mackenzie River and was scrapped in 1899. Captain Smith was the first captain to take his boat down the Mackenzie River and across the Arctic circle. A year previously, in 1898, the Hudson's Bay Company had constructed a second *Wrigley*.

Hudson's Bay Company paddlewheeler, the Wrigley, *at the junction of the Mackenzie and Liard Rivers, 1,200 miles north of Edmonton. Saskatchewan Archives.*

The *Mackenzie River* was built by the Hudson's
Bay Company at Fort Smith, Alberta, in 1911.
Its hull was 126 feet long, 26 feet wide, five feet
deep and could carry over 100 tons of cargo.
The *Mackenzie River* was unusual in that its hull
had a steel frame. While many Mackenzie
steamers had only a wooden hull, and were
built with green lumber at that, this sternwheeler could be replanked and it was, several
times. The *Mackenzie River* operated between
Fort Smith and the Mackenzie River Delta. In
1944, it was wrecked by ice.

The Mackenzie River, *Fort Smith, Alberta,*
c. 1911. Hudson's Bay Company Library.

The *Distributor* was the third boat of this name.
The other two vessels steamed the rivers of the
interior of British Columbia. It was built by the
Hudson's Bay Company at Fort Smith in the
Northwest Territories in 1920. One hundred
and fifty-one feet long, with a 35-foot beam
and six-foot depth, and registered at 876 tons,
it was by far the largest of the three.

   The *Distributor* gave regular service between
Fort Smith and the Mackenzie River until it
was abandoned at Fort Smith in 1946. Its
paddle wheel can be seen in the town park.

Hudson's Bay Company supply boat, the
Distributor, *on the Mackenzie River, c. 1926.*
Hudson's Bay Company Library.

The era of steamboats in the West Coast began in March of 1836 when the Hudson's Bay Company *Beaver* arrived, and ended in 1957 when the *Moyie* was retired from service. In the interim, over three hundred boats had travelled the 572,000 square mile area of British Columbia and the Yukon Territories.

The rivers of British Columbia all drain from the Rocky Mountains, forming lakes, waterfalls and rapids on their way to the Pacific Ocean. As with other Canadian rivers, they are not navigable along their entire length, but only in intermittent sections of a few hundred miles each.

In the southeast of the province, the rivers come together in the Kootenay Lake System. The Kootenay River can be followed all the way into the state of Idaho. To the west, the Columbia River and a series of lakes, the Arrow Lake System, run from the province into the state of Washington.

The mountains of the west coast give rise to rivers which empty into the Pacific. In the south the Fraser and Thompson rivers lead to the port of Vancouver.

In 1858 the Fraser River yielded up some two million dollars in treasure; the Gold Rush was on! With it came the first steamboats on the Fraser, all of them American owned. The very first was the California Steam Navigation Company's *Surprise,* in June of 1858. It was a sidewheeler with two paddlewheels, one on each side of the boat. This type of construction made the boat vulnerable to damage in narrow channels, and from overhanging riverbanks. Moreover, sidewheelers needed a wharf to land at, and such docking facilities were scarce in the early days out west.

Sternwheelers were obviously a better design for the shallow waters of British Columbia. The pioneer sternwheeler on the Fraser was the *Umatilla,* in July of 1858. It plumetted over the Columbia Rapids on its maiden voyage, killing a passenger, but went on to become the first sternwheeler to explore Harrison River and the first to reach the upriver community of Yale.

The bluff-bowed vessels popularly associated with the Mississippi River were in fact used more in British Columbia than anywhere else in North America. Their great advantage was their extremely shallow draught. On the Thompson River, the *Kamloops* worked in eight inches of water. On the Columbia the *Duchess* sailed so close to the bottom that the gravel ridges formed by spawning salmon were obstacles.

As in other parts of Canada, competition for control of the rivers was fierce. No one ever succeeded in getting an exclusive charter for British Columbia waters, however, as the authorities were concerned to keep freight prices down. Businessmen sometimes resorted to building their own ships in defense against the overly high rates of the large companies.

The rivers of British Columbia are not as prone to terrible storms and freezing weather as are the Great Lakes. Consequently there are not so many tales of great marine disasters from this part of the country. One exception to

Wreck of the Beaver. *Public Archives of Canada, PA 29585.*

the rule is the story of the *Enterprise,* which was frozen between Fort Hope and Fort Langley in the freakishly cold winter of 1858. The boat had neither food nor accommodation for its passengers, so many people abandoned ship and tried to walk overland to Fort Langley. Three days later the steamboat broke through the ice, and proceeded along the river, picking up the frost-bitten, weary and ill passengers. Everyone was saved.

For the most part however, local accidents were much less spectacular. The steamboats of British Columbia hit rocks and sank more often than did their counterparts on the Great Lakes. However, as they only sank in four to ten feet of water, the passengers could easily swim to shore! Sinking was considered an occupational hazard rather than a catastrophe. On one trip along the seven-mile-long Giscome Rapids, the *Quesnel* had its hull broken through in fifteen places. The usual remedy for this was to simply patch up the holes with soft material, and keep going. The typical patching material was oakum, which was held in place by a post wedged against the deck. If this was not handy, sacks of anything pliable from the cargo were used as a plug. Even in bad cases, the boats could usually be repaired in a few weeks.

The most dramatic disasters were boiler explosions. Often these were inadvertent, but sometimes a boat, racing against the clock or a rival, would simply build up too much pressure. The engineers would readjust the safety valves so as to go faster; in one instance, a Chief Engineer was so afraid of what might happen that he jumped overboard!

Of the rivalry on the rivers, the Victoria *Colonist* commented: "[it] is becoming fast and furious, and we would advise caution on all sides, for should a disaster occur, a terrible responsibility will attach somewhere."

There are six vessels registered in Canada with the name *Beaver*. Of these six, the one which was built in Victoria, B.C., in 1898, was a sternwheeler and the rest were sidewheelers.

The vessel in our photograph was built at Blackwall on the Thames River, in England, in 1835. Its hull was 101 feet long, 22 feet wide, by 11 feet deep, and registered at approximately 159 tons. It was the first steam vessel on the Pacific coast of Canada and was wrecked just outside the harbour of Vancouver, July 26, 1888.

The builder was Green, Wigram and Green. The two side lever engines had cylinders 35 inches in diameter, with a three-foot stroke. The boiler operated under a steam pressure of 2½ pounds per square inch and developed 70 horsepower. The paddle wheels were 13 feet in diameter. This machinery was manufactured by Boulton and Watt in London, England. The vessel was able to attain a speed of nine miles an hour.

The *Beaver* was launched on May 2, 1835, and, on June 28, it had a trial cruise in the English Channel. It was built as a paddle wheel steamer but the paddle wheel mechanism had not yet been installed.

The *Beaver* left England on September 13, 1835, sailed across the Atlantic Ocean, around Cape Horn, and up the Pacific coast of South and North America.

It arrived at Fort Vancouver, April 10, 1836; the trip had taken 225 days. The fitting of the paddle wheels, guards and attachment to the engine took about a month-and-a-half. On May 31, 1836, the *Beaver* made its first trip up the Pacific coast. From then on it was a freight and trading vessel for the Hudson's Bay Company. Among its captains were Henry Saunders and George Rudlin.

In 1846, after the boundary dispute with the United States, the home port of the *Beaver* was

The sidewheeler, Beaver, *in Vancouver Harbour, c. 1870. Metropolitan Toronto Library Board.*

transferred from Fort Vancouver to Fort Victoria. In 1853, it was joined by a sister ship, the *Otter*, which arrived from England. In 1859 still another ship was added, the *Labouchere*. Because of the salt water, the *Beaver* required new boilers to be installed in 1842 and, again, in 1856. The *Beaver* was to receive a total of six new boilers before it was wrecked.

Finally in 1874, the *Beaver* was sold to a syndicate of seven Victoria businessmen. From then on, it worked around the port of Victoria as a tug and freight transfer.

In July, 1888, the *Beaver* ran aground on Prospect Point outside of Vancouver Harbour, was judged to be beyond salvage and abandoned by its owner. From then on, souvenir hunters stripped the hulk. The boilers were later hauled ashore and preserved in Tacoma, Washington.

William Irving was born in Scotland. In 1849, he sailed to San Francisco where he engaged in the Oregon and California lumber trade until 1859. He and his wife moved to Victoria where he became interested in Fraser River steamers, making his first trip in 1861. In 1862 he built his first steamer, the *Reliance*; in 1864, his second, the *Onward*. He became part-owner of many other steamers before his death on August 28, 1872, at the age of 56.

Mrs. Irving and their son John then took over the shipping business and it became known as the Pioneer Shipping Company. Later on, its assets were acquired by R. P. Rithet, and it became the Canadian Pacific Navigation Company. A few years later, it was taken over again, this time by the Canadian Pacific Railway.

The son, John, took command of his father's boats and when he was only 20, was pilot and captain of the *Onward*. Under John Irving's management, numerous steamers were added to the fleet: *Lillooet*, the *Hope*, the *Glenora*, the *Onward* and the *Royal City* among others.

Captain Irving expected a new transportation boom to start in 1880, and to prepare for it, he built the *William Irving* at Bernard Inlet. The keel was laid on February 1, 1880, and the boat was launched on March 19. This was the largest and best sternwheeler ever to appear on the Fraser River. The length of the hull was 146 feet, the beam 34 feet, and the depth, four feet. The cylinders of the engine were 18 inches in diameter, their stroke six feet. It could develop 74 horsepower. The capacity of the boat was 300 tons and, when fully-loaded, it had a draught of three feet six inches.

The *William Irving* ran on the lower Fraser River and the fare was $3 for a cabin to Yale. Deck passage was $1. On one trip in November, the *William Irving* carried the largest cargo ever taken to Yale, 270 tons. It ended its days

wrecked at New Westminster on June 30, 1894.

The William Irving *at Yale, B.C., 1868. British Columbia Archives.*

The sidewheeler *Amelia* was built in San Francisco in 1863 for the Sacramento River trade. It was 150 feet long, and 26 feet wide and nine deep. The engine had a cylinder three feet in diameter and a stroke of six feet.

The *Amelia* was bought by a new company, the People's Steam Navigation Company, incorporated May 1, 1884.

It arrived at Victoria on June 3, 1884, and ten days later, flying the British flag, began operations on the Victoria, Nanaimo route in fierce competition with the *R. P. Rithet*. Both charged 25 cents for the round trip. For the next two years, the *Amelia* remained on the route, commanded by Captain McCulloch.

It was sold July 17, 1889, at auction, to Captain J. G. Cox. A year later it was sold again—to the Canadian Pacific Navigation Company, which owned it until it was scrapped in 1892.

George S. Rice placed an order for the sidewheeler *Olympia* with John English and Sons, boatbuilders, in New York City. It arrived in San Francisco on November 19, 1868, taking 75 days for the trip from New York. The *Olympia* was 184 feet long, with a 30-foot beam, and a 13-foot hold. Its hull was constructed throughout of seasoned white oak.

It arrived in Vancouver on December 3, and made its first trip to Victoria four days later. In July, 1871, the *Olympia* steamed back to San Francisco where various California steamers paid its owner a subsidy so that he would not run it and interfere with their business.

In 1872, it made a voyage to Honolulu and, later, back to Humboldt, Alaska. In 1873 it was taken out of commission. In 1878, the owners brought the *Olympia* back to Puget

Previous Page Top:
The Amelia, *docked at Broadway Wharf, San Francisco, 1865. British Columbia Archives.*

Previous Page Bottom:
The Princess Louise, *formerly the* Olympia, *at Masset, Queen Charlotte Islands, B.C. British Columbia Archives.*

Right:
The Western Slope *on the Fraser River, c. 1880. British Columbia Archives.*

Sound where it made trips to Victoria and Puget Sound ports. However, business at this time was very poor.

In October, 1878, the Hudson's Bay Company purchased the *Olympia* for $75,000. It made its last voyage under the name *Olympia* to Wrangel, Alaska, in May, 1879, and on its return was renamed the *Princess Louise*. It was registered at the Port of London, England, by its new owners and continued to run out of Victoria until the Canadian Pacific Navigation Company absorbed the steamboat properties of the Hudson's Bay Company.

In 1916, the hull of the *Princess Louise* was in use as a barge by the Vancouver Dredging and Salvage Company which had acquired it from the CPR in 1906. It was purchased in 1916 by the Britannia Mining and Smelting Company which used it to carry ore from Tacoma, Washington. In 1907, the hull was purchased by the Whalen Pulp and Paper Mills. It was beached and abandoned at Woodfibre, B.C., across the Sound from Britannia Beach.

This beautiful sternwheeler, the *Western Slope*, was built in Victoria, B.C., in 1879, with a hull 156 feet long, a 27-foot beam and an eight-foot depth.

The *Western Slope* was built by Captain William Moore and intended for use on the Stikine River. Competition was very stiff on the River at that time and in order to get more speed and more power out of their engines, many of the river boat captains would run their boilers at a higher than legal pressure.

Captain Moore, on June 15, 1881, was summoned to appear in court in New Westminster to answer to a charge that he had run the *Western Slope* at greater than the legal steam pressure. His chief engineer, who had recently been fired, was in court and testified that Moore had arranged that the steam gauge on his boilers should register 40 pounds lower than the actual pressure.

Also, Moore had wedged shut one of the safety valves on his boiler. The only way this valve could release excessive steam pressure was by blowing out the floor of the cabin above it. Other safety valves had been screwed so tightly shut that even with 40% excessive pressure in the boilers, the safety valve did not open up.

Captain Moore and his engineer were fined $2 each. This was a very dangerous practice, quite common on the British Columbia river boats, and it led to many explosions and much loss of life.

Ladies' cabin, the R.P. Rithet, *later the* Baramba, *c. 1882. British Columbia Archives.*

The R. P. Rithet *at Yale, B.C., c. 1882. British Columbia Archives.*

The *R. P. Rithet* was built at New Westminster, B.C. by R. P. Rithet in 1882. Its hull was 117 feet long, 34 feet wide and nine feet deep. It was one of the first vessels equipped with electric lights, a dazzling sight to behold. Its salons were beautifully carved and gilded.

On July 28, 1885 the sidewheeler *Enterprise* collided with the *R. P. Rithet* in the open sea in broad daylight. Captain Insley of the *Rithet* was held responsible. Two people and 24 cattle drowned. In 1887, the *R. P. Rithet* was making regular calls along the Fraser River.

In 1909, it was rebuilt, renamed the *Baramba*, and continued on the same route until 1915, when the superstructure was removed and the hull used as a barge.

The *Kokanee* was launched at Nelson, B.C. on April 7, 1896, for the Columbia and Kootenay Navigation Company. It was 143 feet long, 25 feet wide and six feet deep. Fully-loaded, it could make 18 miles per hour. It ran on the Kootenay Lake System with the steamer *Kuskanook*. In 1923, it became a floating hotel, the main lodge of a hunting and fishing camp.

The Kokanee *at Nelson, B.C., July 2, 1896. British Columbia Archives.*

The Kokanee *dining room, c. 1900. The doors from the first class cabins open directly into this room. British Columbia Archives.*

The Canadian Pacific Railway owned a large number of sternwheelers in British Columbia and one of these was the *Slocan I*. It was launched in 1897 at Rosebery as a sister ship to the *Rossland* for service on Slocan Lake, a waterway between Arrow and Kootenay lakes. It was 150 feet long, 25 feet wide, seven feet deep. It was scrapped in 1905, and the *Slocan II*, probably using the same plans, was built that same year at Rosebery. After years of service, the *Slocan II* was abandoned on Slocan Lake in 1927.

The salon on the Slocan I, *c. 1897. British Columbia Archives.*

The C.P.R. steamer Slocan II *on Slocan Lake, c. 1915. British Columbia Archives.*

The shipyards at Nakusp, B.C., produced several famous sternwheelers, among them the *Rossland*, launched in 1898. It was 183 feet long, 29 feet wide, and seven feet deep and could travel 20 miles per hour when loaded. It joined the Arrow Lakes Service on November 18, 1898. It made the Arrowhead to Robinson run, a 250-mile round trip, within 24 hours. During a heavy storm on January 25, 1917, the *Rossland* foundered at her moorings at Nakusp.

Above Right:
C.P.R. sternwheeler, the Rossland, *on Arrow Lake, B.C. Public Archives of Canada, C 21044.*

Top Right:
The Moyie *observation room. British Columbia Archives.*

Bottom Right:
The Moyie *smoking room. British Columbia Archives.*

The *Moyie* was originally built by the Bertram Ironworks in Toronto with a hull 162 feet long and 30 feet wide for the CPR in 1897. Over one thousand pieces were shipped from Toronto to Vancouver, then Nelson, B.C., in railway freight cars.

The CPR originally intended to build twenty sternwheelers to provide transportation over an all-Canadian route up the Stikine River to the Yukon gold fields. However, because federal government subsidies never materialized, the Stikine River Route was abandoned.

The first voyage of the *Moyie* took place December 7, 1898, when it inaugurated the passenger service connecting the British Columbia Southern Railway from Alberta to the Kootenay Lake region. For over 59 years it sailed between Nelson and Lardeau on Kootenay Lake.

The *Moyie* made its last run on April 27, 1957. It stopped at all its regular ports: Queen's Bay, Kootenay Bay, Walkers Landing, Riondel, Ainsworth, Mirror Lake, Birchdale, Lardeau and Johnsons Landing, a voyage of 87 miles taking nine hours. The *Moyie* was taken over by the Kootenay Lake Historical Society and is now preserved in a concrete berth at the end of Front Street in Kaslo, B.C.

Picnickers disembarking from the Moyie. *British Columbia Archives.*

The British Columbia Express Company owned the sternwheeler, *Operator*, built in Victoria in 1909. It was 138 feet long, 31 feet wide and five feet deep. The *Operator* originally ran on the Skeena River but when that portion of the railway line was completed, it was moved to the Fort George route.

The *Operator* was one of the largest vessels on the Upper Fraser River. In 1912, it could carry over 200 passengers and over 200 tons of freight, while pushing a barge loaded with another 100 tons. It ran from south Fort George to Tête-Jaune Cache, a small community near the head waters of the Fraser River. The *Operator*'s sister ships were the *Conveyor* and the *Omineca*.

The *Operator* sailed down the coast in 1911 and was dismantled at Victoria. Its machinery

The Operator *at the wharf at Tête Jaune Cache, B.C. E. Brown Collection, Alberta Archives.*

was installed in two new sternwheelers at Tête-Jaune Cache.

A second *Operator* was built in Yellowhead, B.C., in 1912, 142 feet long, 35 feet wide, five feet deep. It was abandoned in Prince George in 1918.

The B.C. Express was built at Soda Creek, B.C., in 1912; it operated between Soda Creek and Fort George on the Upper Fraser River. Lacking business it was drawn up on shore in 1914. However, in 1919, the B.X. struck a reef five miles below Fort George Canyon. The Express was overhauled and recaulked in three weeks by a shipyard crew from Victoria to replace it.

When operating in the Grand Canyon area, going against the current of the Upper Fraser River, the roaring furnaces of the Express would gobble up five cords of wood an hour, belching black smoke and live steam from its stack as it made a mighty surge of power against the current.

Captain I. P. Bucey commanded the Express. He was a man of great experience, having learned his trade on the Mississippi, the Columbia, the Yukon, and from perhaps 14 years on the Skeena River.

With the close of the 1920 season, the mail subsidy was not renewed. Both the B.X. and the Express were dismantled, their machinery, boilers and equipment were shipped to Northern Alaska for use by the Alberta and Arctic Transportation Company. The hull and super-structures, abandoned on the riverbank, were eventually carried away by flood waters.

The famous and reliable sternwheeler, Delta King, was built in Glasgow, Scotland, taken apart, and reassembled at Stockton, California in 1925–6. It had a 285-foot-long Swedish steel hull, decks of oak, panels of teak, mahogany, cedar and walnut. Its companion boat was the Delta Queen. They cost $1 million each and were used on the Sacramento to San Francisco run, a memorable overnight cruise in the 1930s. The advent of good roads and the Great Depression caused them to be laid up for a few

The B.C. Express *passing through the Grand Canyon of the Fraser River. British Columbia Archives.*

years. The Delta Queen was taken to the Mississippi River. The Delta King served as a navy ship on San Francisco Bay during World War II.

In 1952, the Aluminum Company of Canada towed the hulk, minus its engines, to Kitimat, 400 miles above Vancouver on the coast of British Columbia, to be used as a bunkhouse for construction workers while they built the smelter.

Seven years later, the hulk was sold again to a group in Stockton, California, who intended to use it as a tourist attraction. These plans never materialized and it sat at the dock, deteriorating. A few years ago, however, it was refurbished. The Delta King steams the Mississippi River, today, as beautiful as ever. Tour information can be found at the back of this book.

The Delta King *on the Mississippi River in the movie* Huckleberry Finn. *The Aluminum Company of Canada.*

The Delta King being used as a dormitory for labourers at Kitimat, B.C. The Aluminum Company of Canada.

Suggested Reading

Barris, Theodore. *Fire Canoe: Prairie Steamboat Days Revisited*, McClelland and Stewart, Toronto, 1977.

Benson, Richard M. *Steamboats and Motorships of the West Coast*, Superior Publishing Company, Seattle, 1968.

Bowen, Dana Thomas. *Lore of the Lakes*, R. E. Publishing, Lachine, Québec, 1969.

_____.*Memories of the Lakes*, R. E. Publishing, Lachine, Québec, 1969.

_____. *Shipwrecks of the Lakes*, R. E. Publishing, Lachine, Québec, 1969.

Brookes, Ivan S. *The Lower St. Lawrence*, Freshwater Press Inc., Cleveland, Ohio, 1974.

Curwood, James Oliver. *The Great Lakes: The Vessels that Plough Them: Their Owners, Their Sailors, and Their Cargoes*, G. P. Putnam's Sons, New York and London, 1909.

Downs, Art. *Paddlewheels on the Frontier: The Story of British Columbia and Yukon Sternwheel Steamers*, Gray's Publishing Ltd., Sidney, B.C., 1972.

Gibbs, Jim. *West Coast Windjammers*, Superior Publishing Company, Seattle, 1968.

Heyl, Eric. *Early American Steamers*, (Vols. I–VI), published by the author at 136 West Oakwood Place, Buffalo, N.Y., 1964.

Legget, Robert. *Ottawa Waterway: Gateway to a Continent*, University of Toronto Press, Toronto, 1975.

Morris, J. A. *Prescott 1810–1967*, The Prescott Journal, Prescott, Ontario, 1969.

Newell, Gordon, and Williamson, John. *Pacific Tug Boats*, Superior Publishing Company, Seattle, 1968.

Peel, Bruce. *Steamboats on the Saskatchewan*, The Western Producer, Saskatoon, 1972.

Tatley, Richard. *Steamboating in Muskoka*, Muskoka Litho., Bracebridge, Ontario, Rev. Ed. 1977.

Wallace, Frederick William. *Wooden Ships and Iron Men*, George Sully and Company, New York, (no date).

Photographs

Photographs may be obtained from the Archives of each province. They are most co-operative and friendly. In addition to these, other excellent sources of pictures are:

C. Patrick Labadie, Curator,
Canal Park Marine Museum,
Duluth, Minnesota,
U.S.A., 55802.

City of Toronto Archives,
James Collection,
New City Hall,
Toronto, Ontario.

Kenneth E. Thro,
Anderson Road, Route 6,
Box 347,
Hayward, Wisconsin,
U.S.A., 56843.

National Photographic and Newspaper Archives of Canada,
Wellington Street,
Ottawa, Canada.

Notman Archives,
McCord Museum,
McGill University,
Montréal, Québec.

Toronto Public Reference Library,
5126 Yonge Street,
Toronto, Ontario.

Societies

Toronto Branch of World Ship Society,
℅ Mr. K. R. Macpherson, 79 Aldershot Crescent, Willowdale, Ontario, Canada, M2P 1M2

The Puget Sound Maritime Historical Society, Seattle, Washington, U.S.A.

The Steamship Historical Society of America, Mrs. Alice S. Wilson, Secretary, 414 Pelton Avenue, Staten Island, New York, U.S.A., 10310.

The World Ship Society,
℅ Mr. J. C. Taylor, 26 The Chase, Thundersley, Benfleet, Essex, SS73BS, England.

Steamboat and Paddle Wheel Information Available From

Huronia Museum,
Midland, Ontario.

The Lake Superior Marine Museum Association,
Canal Park,
Duluth, Minnesota,
U.S.A., 55802.

Marine Museum,
Collingwood, Ontario.

Marine Museum,
Exhibition Park,
Toronto, Ontario.

Marine Museum,
Kingston, Ontario.

Marine Museum,
Port Colborne, Ontario.

National Maritime Museum,
Greenwich SE 10,
London, England.

Science Museum,
London, England.

Shelburne Museum,
Shelburne, Vermont,
U.S.A., 05482.

Paddle Wheel Museums

CANADA:

Argenteuil Museum
Carillon, Québec.

Sicamous, a sternwheeler, has been beached on Lake Okanagan, Penticton, British Columbia, and is open for inspection.

U.S.A.:

Greenfield Village & Henry Ford Museum,
Dearborn, Michigan,
U.S.A., 48121.
Sternwheeler *Swanee* on view, and rides.

Julius C. Wilkie Steamboat Museum,
% Dr. L. I. Younger,
Winona, Minnesota,
U.S.A., 55987.

Keokuk River Museum,
226 High Street,
Keokuk, Iowa,
U.S.A., 52632.
Sternwheeler *George M. Verity* on view.

Shelburne Museum Inc.
Shelburne, Vermont,
U.S.A., 05482.
Sidewheeler *Ticonderoga* on view.

Paddlewheelers Still Operating

Belle of Louisville,
Foot of Fourth Street,
Louisville, Kentucky,
U.S.A., 40202.

Delta Queen,
Green Line Steamers Inc.,
322 E. Fourth Street,
Cincinnati, Ohio,
U.S.A., 45202.

Lake George Steamboat Co. Inc.,
P.O. Box 551,
Lake George, N.Y.,
U.S.A., 12845.

Trillium, Toronto Parks Department,
Ferry Service, Toronto Harbour,
Toronto, Ontario.

Moyie, (a half-sized replica of the original, diesel-powered sternwheeler), travels on Glenmore Lake with 180 passengers. Information from the Heritage Park Society, 1900 Heritage Drive, Calgary, Alberta, Canada, T2V 2X3.

People in Ontario are very fortunate in that they have in their vicinity two paddle wheel steamboats.

The *Trillium*, shown on our cover, is an excellent example of a sidewheeled boat with an inclined acting steam engine. It was launched in June, 1910, by the Toronto Ferry Company and was not retired until 1956. On July 25, 1957, it was proposed that the vessel, which was no longer being used, be converted to a garbage scow. However on September 17, 1957, it was towed to a Toronto Island lagoon where it remained for sixteen years. On two occasions, it sank to the bottom of the lagoon because someone had left the garbage port open and water filled the vessel. On both occasions it was raised but continued to deteriorate until most of the wooden superstructure was rotted. It was rescued from the scrapyard by the Toronto Parks Commission in 1973, rebuilt, and returned to service in 1976.

Second is a sternwheeler which began life on the Mississippi River around 1898. After a useful life, it was laid up, then was transported to Buffalo, New York, where it became a restaurant. Now in Mississauga, Ontario, it is the Showboat Restaurant. It is brightly lit and brightly painted, but its heart has been removed. The boilers and the firebox are gone from the engine room and, in their place, (where once strong men shovelled coal into a roaring furnace and mighty boilers built up pressure) there is an oval bar and a mini-skirted waitress asking, "Drinks Sir?" On each side of the bar are the remnants of the pistons and the steam condensing chests, painted a garish red. The piston rods have been cut and used for scrap, the pipes have been removed, and a powerful electric motor now drives the paddle wheel to entertain the dining guests. The dining room is splendid, probably authentically reproduced, and well worth the visit.

Registration

In the early 1800s in Canada, there were few official registries for ships; thus, information on old boats can only be obtained from old insurance company records, or records that may have been kept at large harbours. Around 1830, if a ship were registered, it would be registered either under the Imperial Merchant Shipping Act of Great Britain or under a separate Act in the Province of Lower Canada. As a consequence, most of the records we find today pertain only to the lower St. Lawrence River area. Very few harbour or port records remain between the Great Lakes and Montréal.

After 1874, the new Dominion of Canada standardized the registration of vessels including methods of measurement. This new system was based on and was part of the British system. Ships transferred from British to Canadian Registry retained their British registration numbers.

The historian's difficulties are compounded by the fact that the authorities in Québec did not assign numbers to vessels when they were registered and no numbers were assigned to these same vessels in the new registry system for the Dominion of Canada.

When a new hull was built it was assigned a permanent registration number which it retained no matter how often a ship was renamed or refitted. However, if the hull and engines were so greatly altered that the vessel was a new ship, the hull was given a new number.

The historian can distinguish between ships and trace the history of various ships through numerous renamings by comparing hull numbers.